MAKING LOVE
TO MARILYN

*From the seduction to the end of the affair
in a collection of sensual love poems*

EDITED BY SUSAN ROBERTS

VIKING

VIKING

Published by the Penguin Group
Penguin Books Ltd, 27 Wrights Lane, London w8 5TZ, England
Penguin Books USA Inc., 375 Hudson Street, New York, New York 10014, USA
Penguin Books Australia Ltd, Ringwood, Victoria, Australia
Penguin Books Canada Ltd, 10 Alcorn Avenue, Toronto, Ontario, Canada M4V 3B2
Penguin Books (NZ) Ltd, 182–190 Wairau Road, Auckland 10, New Zealand

Penguin Books Ltd, Registered Offices: Harmondsworth, Middlesex, England

This collection first published 1997
10 9 8 7 6 5 4 3 2 1

Introduction and selection copyright © Susan Roberts, 1997
The Acknowledgements on pages 170–73 constitute an extension of this
copyright page

Set in 10/13pt Monotype Sabon
Typeset by Cambridge Photosetting Services
Printed in Great Britain by Clays International Ltd, St Ives plc

A CIP catalogue record for this book is available from the British Library

ISBN 0–670–87195–8

CONTENTS

THE SEVEN YEAR ITCH 107

I'M THROUGH WITH LOVE 139

INTRODUCTION

Marilyn Monroe intrigues us still. For men and women alike, she has come to embody many ideas and experiences of love, everything from innocence to scandal, from seduction to tragedy. Hers is an image which endures, even strengthens with time. In another 2,000 years she may well take her place alongside Aphrodite.

This anthology began its life as a radio series, and it is a testament to the actress's power that the Radio 4 commissioner at the time fondly called *Making Love to Marilyn* the series title of the year. It was broadcast at midnight, in the hope, no doubt, of adding naturally to the Radio 4 audience!

When it came to broadcasting the selection of what could be called sensuous love poems on the radio, it seemed appropriate to employ Marilyn Monroe as a means of holding them together. Readings of the poems, by both poets and actors, were interspersed with recordings of her songs and extracts from the soundtracks of her films. These have also provided the section titles for the book. With her help, this collection, like the radio programmes, works its way along a familiar but not inevitable path, from the seduction, 'I Wanna be Loved by You', to the end of the affair, 'I'm Through with Love'.

Like the best seductions, the best poetry about lovemaking is often suggestive and oblique rather than explicit. A water-pump frozen in winter may seem an unlikely subject for a love poem, but in Seamus Heaney's hands it becomes an exciting metaphor. At the other end of the scale, even though most blue or bawdy verse has been passed over, more direct depictions and a frisson of eroticism are included. What could be more passionate than Ted Hughes's description of a man and woman exploring and building each other in 'Bride and Groom Lie Hidden for Three Days'?

The poems in the first three sections of the book have been chosen for their sensuality, for their relish and enjoyment of the passion of love, whether in an exotic or more down-to-earth context. These are poems to enjoy. They fizz on the page, whether in a fantasy of anticipation:

> Filling her compact & delicious body
> with chicken paprika, she glanced at me
> twice.
>> (4th song *from* '77 Dream Songs' by John Berryman)

or of a love that's unfulfilled:

> My love is as a fever, longing still
> For that which longer nurseth the disease;
>> ('Sonnet 147' by William Shakespeare)

or the act of making love:

> Licence my roving hands, and let them go
> Before, behind, between, above, below.
>> ('To His Mistress Going to Bed' by John Donne)

As well as sobriety and contemplation, there's room for more than just a little humour. Love, after all, has its funny side. Whether encouraging a wry smile, a belly-laugh or a tear, these poems describe many moods, reflecting the sometimes playful, sometimes passionate, sometimes ludicrous world of sexual love:

Sex suppressed will go berserk,
But it keeps us all alive.
It's a wonderful change from wives and work
And it ends at half past five.

('Office Friendships' by Gavin Ewart)

In the last two sections, a sourer note creeps in, as 'The Seven Year Itch' leads to 'I'm Through with Love'. But alongside the bitterness of betrayals and endings there's the sweetness of memory and reflection, the sadness of loss and the mourning for a time that's gone.

And in my heart there stirs a quiet pain
For unremembered lads that not again
Will turn to me at midnight with a cry.

('What Lips My Lips Have Kissed' by Edna St Vincent Millay)

The theme of love has resonance for us all; for poets, always in search of the everlasting poem, it's an essential and enduring one. Between these pages are poems written around 600 BC by Sappho; they are as relevant to us today as those written recently by Peter Reading or Selima Hill. This is why the poems are arranged by theme rather than chronologically. You'll find Homer alongside Ezra Pound and Carol Ann Duffy alongside C. P. Cavafy, and I hope you'll enjoy the shadows they cast over each other. There's also a progression through the book, a loose story, for anyone choosing to read from beginning to end.

SUSAN ROBERTS

I WANNA BE LOVED BY YOU

Stand up and look at me face to face,
                                                friend to friend;
unfurl the loveliness in your eyes

SAPPHO *translated by Josephine Balmer*

LYNN PETERS

I Suspect

I suspect
There would be more poems
About sex
If it rhymed with more than
Pecks
Necks
Erects and ejects.

This begins to sound promising.
I may write one.

WENDY COPE

Verse for a Birthday Card

Many happy returns and good luck
When it comes to a present, I'm stuck.
    If you weren't far away
    On your own special day,
I could give you a really nice glass of lager.

JOHN BERRYMAN

4th Song from 77 Dream Songs

Filling her compact & delicious body
with chicken paprika, she glanced at me
twice.
Fainting with interest, I hungered back
and only the fact of her husband & four other people
kept me from springing on her

or falling at her little feet and crying
'You are the hottest one for years of night
Henry's dazed eyes
have enjoyed, Brilliance.' I advanced upon
(despairing) my spumoni – Sir Bones: is stuffed,
de world, wif feeding girls.

– Black hair, complexion Latin, jewelled eyes
downcast . . . The slob beside her feasts . . . What wonders
is she sitting on, over there?
The restaurant buzzes. She might as well be on Mars.
Where did it all go wrong? There ought to be a law against
    Henry.
– Mr Bones: there is.

SAPPHO *translated by Mary Barnard*

He is more than a hero

He is more than a hero

He is a god in my eyes –
the man who is allowed
to sit beside you – he

who listens intimately
to the sweet murmur of
your voice, the enticing

laughter that makes my own
heart beat fast. If I meet
you suddenly, I can't

speak – my tongue is broken;
a thin flame runs under
my skin; seeing nothing,

hearing only my own ears
drumming, I drip with sweat;
trembling shakes my body

and I turn paler than
dry grass. At such times
death isn't far from me

SIMON ARMITAGE

You May Turn Over and Begin . . .

'Which of these films was Dirk Bogarde
not in? One hundredweight of bauxite

makes how much aluminium?
How many tales in *The Decameron*?'

General Studies, the upper sixth, a doddle, a cinch
for anyone with an ounce of common sense

or a calculator
with a memory feature.

Having galloped through but not caring enough
to check or double-check, I was dreaming of

milk-white breasts and nakedness, or more specifically
virginity.

That term – everybody felt the heat
but the girls were having none of it:

long and cool like cocktails,
out of reach, their buns and pigtails

only let out for older guys with studded jackets
and motor-bikes and spare helmets.

One jot of consolation
was the tall spindly girl riding pillion

on her man's new Honda
who, with the lights at amber,

put down both feet and stood to stretch her limbs,
to lift the visor and push back her fringe

and to smooth her tight jeans.
As he pulled off down the street

she stood there like a wishbone,
high and dry, her legs wide open,

and rumour has it he didn't notice
till he came round in the ambulance

having underbalanced on a tight left-hander.
A *Taste of Honey*. Now I remember.

GAVIN EWART

Office Friendships

Eve is madly in love with Hugh
And Hugh is keen on Jim.
Charles is in love with very few
And few are in love with him.

Myra sits typing notes of love
With romantic pianist's fingers.
Dick turns his eyes to the heavens above
Where Fran's divine perfume lingers.

Nicky is rolling eyes and tits
And flaunting her wiggly walk.
Everybody is thrilled to bits
By Clive's suggestive talk.

Sex suppressed will go berserk,
But it keeps us all alive.
It's a wonderful change from wives and work
And it ends at half past five.

CHARLOTTE LENNOX

from *The Art of Coquetry*

First form your artful looks with studious care,
From mild to grave, from tender to severe.
Oft on the careless youth your glances dart,
A tender meaning let each glance impart.
Whene'er he meet your looks, with modest pride
And soft confusion turn your eyes aside,
Let a soft sigh steal out, as if by chance,
Then cautious turn, and steal another glance.
Caught by these arts, with pride and hope elate,
The destined victim rushes on his fate:
Pleased, his imagined victory pursues,
And the kind maid with soft attention views,
Contemplates now her shape, her air, her face,
And thinks each feature wears an added grace;

Till gratitude, which first his bosom proves,
By slow degrees sublimed, at length he loves.
'Tis harder still to fix than gain a heart;
What's won by beauty must be kept by art.
Too kind a treatment the blest lover cloys,
And oft despair the growing flame destroys:
Sometimes with smiles receive him, sometimes tears,
And wisely balance both his hopes and fears.
Perhaps he mourns his ill-requited pains,
Condemns your sway, and strives to break his chains;
Behaves as if he now your scorn defied,
And thinks at least he shall alarm your pride:
But with indifference view the seeming change,
And let your eyes to seek new conquests range;

While his torn breast with jealous fury burns,
He hopes, despairs, adores and hates by turns;
With anguish now repents the weak deceit,
And powerful passion bears him to your feet.

HUGO WILLIAMS

Toilet

I wonder will I speak to the girl
sitting opposite me on this train.
I wonder will my mouth open and say,
'Are you going all the way
to Newcastle?' or 'Can I get you a coffee?'
Or will it simply go 'aaaaah'
as if it had a mind of its own?

Half closing eggshell blue eyes,
she runs her hand through her hair
so that it clings to the carriage cloth;
then slowly frees itself.
She finds a brush and her long fair hair
flies back and forth like an African fly-whisk,
making me feel dizzy.

Suddenly, without warning,
she packs it all away in a rubber band
because I have forgotten to look out
the window for a moment.
A coffee is granted permission
to pass between her lips
and does so eagerly, without fuss.

A tunnel finds us looking out the window
into one another's eyes. She leaves her seat,
but I know that she likes me
because the light saying 'TOILET'
has come on, a sign that she is lifting
her skirt, taking down her pants
and peeing all over my face.

GEORGE CRABBE

Peter Pratt, the gardener

from *The Parish Register, Part II*

Not Darwin's self had more delight to sing
Of floral courtship, in th' awaken'd spring,
Than Peter Pratt, who simpering loves to tell
How rise the stamens, as the pistils swell;
How bend and curl the moist-top to the spouse,
And give and take the vegetable vows;
How those esteem'd of old but tips and chives,
Are tender husbands and obedient wives;
Who live and love within the sacred bower, –
That bridal bed, the vulgar term a flower.
  Hear Peter proudly, to some humble friend,
A wondrous secret, in his science, lend:
'Would you advance the nuptial hour and bring
The fruit of autumn with the flowers of spring;
View that light frame where Cucumis lies spread,
And trace the husbands in their golden bed,
Three powder'd anthers; then no more delay,
But to the stigma's tip their dust convey;
Then by thyself, from prying glance secure,
Twirl the full tip and make your purpose sure;
A long-abiding race the deed shall pay,
Nor one unblest abortion pine away.'

PUBLIUS OVIDIUS NASO (OVID) *translated by
John Oldham*

That he loves women of all sorts and sizes

from the *Amores*

Not I, I never vainly durst pretend
My Follies and my Frailties to defend:
I own my Faults, if it avail to own,
While like a graceless wretch I still go on:
I hate my self, but yet in spite of Fate
Am fain to be that loathed thing I hate:
In vain I would shake off this load of Love,
Too hard to bear, yet harder to remove:
I want the strength my fierce Desires to stem,
Hurried away by the impetuous stream.
'Tis not one Face alone subdues my Heart,
But each wears Charms, and every Eye a Dart:
And wheresoe're I cast my Looks abroad,
In every place I find Temptations strow'd.
The modest kills me with her down-cast Eyes,
And Love his ambush lays in that disguise.
The Brisk allures me with her gaity,
And shews how Active she in bed will be:
If Coy, like cloyster's Virgins, she appears,
She but dissembles, what she most desires:
If she be vers'd in Arts, and deeply read,
I long to get a Learned Maidenhead:
Or if Untaught and Ignorant she be,
She takes me then with her simplicity:

One likes my Verses, and commends each Line,
And swears that *Cowley's*[1] are but dull to mine:
Her in mere Gratitude I must approve,
For who, but would his kind Applauder love?
Another damns my Poetry, and me,
And plays the Critick most judiciously:
And she too fires my Heart, and she too charms,
And I'm agog to have her in my arms.
One with her soft and wanton Trip does please,
And prints in every step, she sets, a Grace:
Another walks with stiff ungainly tread;
But she may learn more pliantness abed.
This sweetly sings; her Voice does Love inspire,
And every Breath kindles and blows the fire:
Who can forbear to kiss those Lips, whose sound
The ravish'd Ears does with such softness wound?
That sweetly plays: and while her Fingers move,
While o're the bounding Strings their touches rove,
My Heart leaps too, and every Pulse beats Love:
What Reason is so pow'rful to withstand
The magick force of that resistless Hand?
Another Dances to a Miracle,
And moves her numerous Limbs with graceful skill:
And she, or else the Devil's in't, must charm,
A touch of her would bed-rid Hermits warm.
If tall; I guess what plenteous Game she'll yield,
Where Pleasure ranges o're so wide a Field:
If low; she's pretty: both alike invite,
The Dwarf, and Giant both my wishes fit.
Undress'd; I think how killing she'd appear,
If arm'd with all Advantages she were:

1 Oldham has substituted his contemporary, the poet Abraham Cowley,
  for Ovid's Callimachus.

Richly attir'd; she's the gay Bait of Love,
And knows with Art to set her Beauties off.
I like the Fair, I like the Red-hair'd one,
And I can find attractions in the Brown:
If curling Jet adorn her snowy Neck,
The beauteous Leda is reported Black:
If curling Gold; Aurora's painted so:
All sorts of Histories my Love does know.
I like the Young with all her blooming Charms,
And Age it self is welcome to my Arms:
There uncropt Beauty in its flow'r assails,
Experience here, and riper sense prevails.
In fine, whatever of the Sex are known
To stock this spacious and well-furnish'd Town;
Whatever any single man can find
Agreeable of all the num'rous kind:
At all alike my haggard Love does fly,
And each is Game, and each a Miss for me.

ANDREW MARVELL

To His Coy Mistress

Had we but world enough, and time,
This coyness, lady, were no crime –
We would sit down and think which way
To walk, and pass our long love's day.
Thou by the Indian Ganges' side
Should'st rubies find; I by the tide
Of Humber would complain. I would
Love you ten years before the Flood,
And you should if you please refuse
Till the Conversion of the Jews.
My vegetable love should grow
Vaster than empires, and more slow.
An hundred years should go to praise
Thine eyes, and on thy forehead gaze;
Two hundred to adore each breast,
But thirty thousand to the rest;
An age at least to every part,
And the last age should show your heart.
For, lady, you deserve this state,
Nor would I love at lower rate.

But at my back I always hear
Time's winged chariot hurrying near;
And yonder all before us lie
Deserts of vast eternity.
Thy beauty shall no more be found,
Nor in thy marble vault shall sound
My echoing song; then worms shall try
That long-preserved virginity,

And your quaint honour turn to dust,
And into ashes all my lust.
The grave's a fine and private place,
But none, I think, do there embrace.

 Now, therefore, while the youthful hue
Sits on thy skin like morning dew,
And while thy willing soul transpires
At every pore with instant fires,
Now let us sport us while we may,
And now, like amorous birds of prey
Rather at once our time devour
Than languish in his slow-chapped power.
Let us roll all our strength, and all
Our sweetness, up into one ball
And tear our pleasures with rough strife
Thorough the iron gates of life.
Thus, though we cannot make our sun
Stand still, yet we will make him run.

CAROL ANN DUFFY

Warming Her Pearls

Next to my own skin, her pearls. My mistress
bids me wear them, warm them, until evening
when I'll brush her hair. At six, I place them
round her cool, white throat. All day I think of her,

resting in the Yellow Room, contemplating silk
or taffeta, which gown tonight? She fans herself
whilst I work willingly, my slow heat entering
each pearl. Slack on my neck, her rope.

She's beautiful. I dream about her
in my attic bed; picture her dancing
with tall men, puzzled by my faint, persistent scent
beneath her French perfume, her milky stones.

I dust her shoulders with a rabbit's foot,
watch the soft blush seep through her skin
like an indolent sigh. In her looking-glass
my red lips part as though I want to speak.

Full moon. Her carriage brings her home. I see
her every movement in my head . . . Undressing,
taking off her jewels, her slim hand reaching
for the case, slipping naked into bed, the way

she always does . . . And I lie here awake,
knowing the pearls are cooling even now
in the room where my mistress sleeps. All night
I feel their absence and I burn.

ANON (4th Century BC)

The Song of the Shulamite

from *The Song of Songs*

My beloved is white and ruddy,
The chiefest among ten thousand.
His head is as the most fine gold,
His locks are bushy, and black as a raven.
His eyes are like doves beside the water brooks;
Washed with milk, and fitly set.
His cheeks are as a bed of spices, as banks of sweet herbs.

His lips are as lilies, dropping liquid myrrh.
His hands are as rings of gold set with beryl:
His body is as ivory work overlaid with sapphires.
His legs are as pillars of marble, set upon sockets of fine
    gold:
His aspect is like Lebanon, excellent as the cedars.
His mouth is most sweet: yea, he is altogether lovely.
This is my beloved, and this is my friend,
O daughters of Jerusalem.

OSCAR WILDE

From a Picture Painted by Miss V. T.

A fair slim boy not made for this world's pain,
With hair of gold thick clustering round his ears,
   And longing eyes half veil'd by foolish tears
Like bluest water seen through mists of rain;
Pale cheeks whereon no kiss hath left its stain,
     Red under-lip drawn in for fear of Love,
     And white throat whiter than the breast of dove –
Alas! Alas! if all should be in vain.
Behind, wide fields, and reapers all a-row
In heat and labour toiling wearily,
To no sweet sound of laughter or of lute.
The sun is shooting wide its crimson glow,
Still the boy dreams: nor knows that night is nigh,
And in the night-time no man gathers fruit.

CHRISTOPHER MARLOWE

from *Hero and Leander*

Leander

Amorous Leander, beautiful and young
(Whose tragedy divine Musaeus sung)
Dwelt at Abydos; since him dwelt there none
For whom succeeding times make greater moan.
His dangling tresses that were never shorn,
Had they been cut, and unto Colchos borne,
Would have allured the venturous youth of Greece
To hazard more than for the Golden Fleece.
Fair Cynthia wished his arms might be her sphere;
Grief makes her pale because she moves not there.
His body was as straight as Circe's wand;
Jove might have sipped out nectar from his hand.
Even as delicious meat is to the taste,
So was his neck in touching, and surpassed
The white of Pelops' shoulder. I could tell ye
How smooth his breast was, and how white his belly,
And whose immortal fingers did imprint
That heavenly path with many a curious dint
That runs along his back, but my rude pen
Can hardly blazon forth the loves of men,
Much less of powerful gods: let it suffice
That my slack muse sings of Leander's eyes,
Those orient cheeks and lips, exceeding his
That leapt into the water for a kiss
Of his own shadow, and despising many,
Died ere he could enjoy the love of any.
Had wild Hippolytus Leander seen,

Enamoured of his beauty had he been;
His presence made the rudest peasant melt,
That in the vast uplandish country dwelt.
The barbarous Thracian soldier, moved with nought,
Was moved with him, and for his favour sought.
Some swore he was a maid in man's attire,
For in his looks were all that men desire,
A pleasant, smiling cheek, a speaking eye,
A brow for love to banquet royally;
And such as knew he was a man would say,
'Leander, thou art made for amorous play:
Why art thou not in love, and loved of all?
Though thou be fair, yet be not thine own thrall.'

THOMAS MOORE

Did Not

'Twas a new feeling – something more
Than we had dared to own before,
    Which then we hid not:
We saw it in each other's eye,
And wished, in every half-breathed sigh,
    To speak, but did not.

She felt my lips' impassioned touch –
'Twas the first time I dared so much,
    And yet she chid me not;
But whispered o'er my burning brow,
'Oh, do you doubt I love you now?'
    Sweet soul! I did not.

Warmly I felt her bosom thrill,
I pressed it closer, closer still,
    Though gently bid not,
Till – oh: the world hath seldom heard
Of lovers, who so nearly erred,
    And yet, who did not.

THOM GUNN

The Hug

It was your birthday, we had drunk and dined
    Half of the night with our old friend
        Who'd showed us in the end
    To a bed I reached in one drunk stride.
        Already I lay snug,
And drowsy with the wine dozed on one side.

I dozed, I slept. My sleep broke on a hug,
        Suddenly, from behind,
In which the full lengths of our bodies pressed:
        Your instep to my heel,
    My shoulder-blades against your chest.
    It was not sex, but I could feel
    The whole strength of your body set,
        Or braced, to mine,
        And locking me to you
    As if we were still twenty-two
    When our grand passion had not yet
        Become familial.
    My quick sleep had deleted all
    Of intervening time and place.
        I only knew
The stay of your secure firm dry embrace.

CAROL ANN DUFFY

Steam

Not long ago so far, a lover and I
in a room of steam –

a sly, thirsty silvery word – lay down,
opposite ends, and vanished.

Quite recently, if one of us sat up,
or stood, or stretched, naked,

a nude pose in soft pencil
behind tissue paper

appeared, rubbed itself out, slow,
with a smokey cloth.

Say a matter of months. This hand reaching
through the steam

to touch the real thing, shockingly there,
not a ghost at all.

E. E. CUMMINGS

i like my body when it is with your

i like my body when it is with your
body. It is so quite new a thing.
Muscles better and nerves more.
i like your body. i like what it does,
i like its hows. i like to feel the spine
of your body and its bones, and the trembling
-firm-smooth ness and which i will
again and again and again
kiss, i like kissing this and that of you,
i like, slowly stroking the, shocking fuzz
of your electric fur, and what-is-it comes
over parting flesh . . . And eyes big love-crumbs,
and possibly i like the thrill
of under me you so quite new

TENNESSEE WILLIAMS

Life Story

After you've been to bed together for the first time,
without the advantage or disadvantage of any prior
    acquaintance,
the other party very often says to you,
Tell me about yourself, I want to know all about you,
what's your story? And you think maybe they really and
    truly do

sincerely want to know your life story, and so you light up
a cigarette and begin to tell it to them, the two of you
lying together in completely relaxed positions
like a pair of rag dolls a bored child dropped on a bed.

You tell them your story, or as much of your story
as time or a fair degree of prudence allows, and they say,
    Oh, oh, oh, oh, oh,
each time a little more faintly, until the oh
is just an audible breath, and then of course

there's some interruption. Slow room service comes up
with a bowl of melting ice cubes, or one of you rises to pee
and gaze at himself with mild astonishment in the
    bathroom mirror.
And then, the first thing you know, before you've had time
to pick up where you left off with your enthralling life
    story,
they're telling you *their* life story, exactly as they'd
    intended to all along,

and you're saying, Oh, oh, oh, oh, oh,
each time a little more faintly, the vowel at last becoming
no more than an audible sigh,
as the elevator, halfway down the corridor and a turn to
      the left,
draws one last, long, deep breath of exhaustion
and stops breathing forever. Then?

Well, one of you falls asleep
and the other one does likewise with a lighted cigarette in
      his mouth,
and that's how people burn to death in hotel rooms.

EMILY DICKINSON

Wild Nights – Wild Nights!
Were I with thee
Wild Nights should be
Our luxury!

Futile – the Winds –
To a Heart in port –
Done with the Compass –
Done with the Chart!

Rowing in Eden –
Ah, the Sea!
Might I but moor – Tonight –
In Thee!

ALAN JENKINS

Storm

At 2 a.m. she arrived out of the wild north wearing
her daffodil-yellow fisherman's coat – with warm
cheeks and a strange smell and swearing up a storm
at the minicab driver who'd tried to get a leg over
and ended by pulling a fast one. A half of Bells,
some fifteen B&H, and she was calm enough
to ferret through my albums with the white-denim furrow
of her tail in the air – at last we got off
on *Louise*, the girl *with perfect skin* and *cheekbones like
geometry* (at which point I brought in her own
perfect skin, and reached to stroke it), then someone else
who *looked like Eve Marie-Saint* and *read Simone
de Beauvoir* – as she does, or did; 'I'm not a dyke,
you know', she said suddenly as she burrowed
deeper into bed, and sleepy-drunk, I was all at sea . . .

PIERRE LOUYS

The Complaisant Friend

from *Chansons de Bilitis*

The storm lasted all night. Selenis, with her lovely
hair, came to spin with me. She stayed for fear of
the mud, and we filled my little bed, clasped close
to each other. When two girls go to bed together, sleep
stays at the door. 'Bilitis, tell me, tell me, whom
do you love?' To caress me softly she slipped her leg
over mine. And over my mouth she said: 'Bilitis, I
know whom you love. Shut your eyes. I am Lycas!'
I answered, touching her: 'Can I not see that you
are a girl? Your pleasantry is out of place.' But
she rejoined: 'I am really Lycas, if you shut your
lids. Here are his arms, and here are his hands . . .'
And in the silence she tenderly delighted my dreaming
with a singular vision.

JOHN AGARD

Blessed Undressed

Blessed you
are undressed.
Blessed undressed.
Obsessed I
for you undressed
will find no rest
till I obsessed
am blessed
by you undressed
and you obsessed
are blessed
by me undressed.
These tongue-twisting words
will put us through
time's tongue-twisting test
till no more no less
no worst no best
no me no you.

Just two creatures
rooting in the soil of heaven.
Blessed, undressed, at rest.

DON'T BOTHER TO KNOCK

[I was dreaming of you but]
just then
Dawn, in her golden sandals
                    [woke me]

SAPPHO *translated by Josephine Balmer*

GRACE NICHOLS

Invitation

I

If my fat
was too much for me
I would have told you
I would have lost a stone
or two

I would have gone jogging
even when it was fogging
I would have weighed in
sitting the bathroom scale
with my tail tucked in

I would have dieted
more care than a diabetic

But as it is
I'm feeling fine
feel no need
to change my lines
when I move I'm target light

Come up and see me sometime

II

Come up and see me sometime
Come up and see me sometime

My breasts are huge exciting
amnions of watermelon
                    your hands can't cup
my thighs are twin seals
                    fat slick pups

there's a purple cherry
below the blues
                    of my black seabelly
there's a mole that gets a ride
each time I shift the heritage
of my behind

Come up and see me sometime

ROBERT GRAVES

Down, Wanton, Down!

Down, wanton, down! Have you no shame
That at the whisper of Love's name,
Or Beauty's, presto! up you raise
Your angry head and stand at gaze?

Poor Bombard-captain, sworn to reach
The ravelin and effect a breach –
Indifferent what you storm or why,
So be that in the breach you die!

Love may be blind, but Love at least
Knows what is man and what mere beast;
Or Beauty wayward, but requires
More delicacy from her squires.

Tell me, my witless, whose one boast
Could be your staunchness at the post,
When were you made a man of parts
To think fine and profess the arts?

Will many-gifted Beauty come
Bowing to your bald rule of thumb,
Or Love swear loyalty to your crown?
Be gone, have done! Down, wanton, down!

SELIMA HILL

Desire's a Desire

It taunts me
like the muzzle of a gun;
it sinks into my soul like chilled honey
packed into the depths of treacherous wounds;
it wraps me up in cold green sheets
like Indian squaws
who wrap their babies in the soft green sheathes of irises
that smell of starch;
it tattooes my shins;
it itches my thighs
like rampant vaginal flora;
it tickles my cheeks
like silkworms munching mulberry leaves
on silk farms;
it nuzzles my plucked armpits like fat dogs;
it plays me
like a piano being played
by regimented fingers
through pressed sheets;
it walks across my back
like geese at dawn,
or the gentle manners
of my only nurse,
who handles me like glass, or Bethlehem.

My skin is white.
I neither eat nor sleep.
My only desire's a desire
to be free from desire.

WILLIAM SHAKESPEARE

Sonnet 147

My love is as a fever, longing still
For that which longer nurseth the disease;
Feeding on that which doth preserve the ill,
The uncertain sickly appetite to please.
My reason, the physician to my love,
Angry that his prescriptions are not kept,
Hath left me, and I desperate now approve
Desire is death, which physic did except.
Past cure am I, now reason is past care,
And frantic-mad with evermore unrest;
My thoughts and my discourse as madmen's are,
At random from the truth vainly expressed.
    For I have sworn thee fair, and thought thee bright,
    Who art as black as hell, as dark as night.

WILLIAM SHAKESPEARE

Sonnet 129

Th' expense of spirit in a waste of shame
Is lust in action; and till action, lust
Is perjur'd, murd'rous, bloody, full of blame,
Savage, extreme, rude, cruel, not to trust;
Enjoy'd no sooner but despised straight;
Past reason hunted, and, no sooner had,
Past reason hated, as a swallowed bait,
On purpose laid to make the taker mad –
Mad in pursuit, and in possession so;
Had, having, and in quest to have, extreme;
A bliss in proof, and prov'd, a very woe;
Before, a joy propos'd; behind, a dream.
    All this the world well knows; yet none knows well
    To shun the heaven that leads men to this hell.

WENDY COPE

from *Strugnell's Sonnets*

The expense of spirits is a crying shame,
So is the cost of wine. What bard today
Can live like old Khayyam? It's not the same –
A loaf and thou and Tesco's Beaujolais.
I had this bird called Sharon, fond of gin –
Could knock back six or seven. At the price
I paid a high wage for each hour of sin
And that was why I only had her twice.
Then there was Tracy, who drank rum and Coke,
So beautiful I didn't mind at first
But love grows colder. Now some other bloke
Is subsidizing Tracy and her thirst.
I need a woman, honest and sincere,
Who'll come across on half a pint of beer.

The Ram

He jangles his keys in the rain
and I follow like a lamb.
His house is as smoky as a dive.
We go straight downstairs to his room.

I lie on his bed and watch him
undress. His orange baseball jacket,
all the way from Ontario,
drops to the floor – THE RAMS, in felt,

arched across the hunky back.
He unzips his calf-length
Star-walkers, his damp black Levi's,
and adjusts his loaded modelling-pouch:

he stands before me in his socks –
as white as bridesmaids,
little daisies, driven snow.
John Wayne watches from the wall

beside a shelf-ful of pistols.
Well, he says, *d'you like it?*
All I can think of is Granny,
how she used to shake her head,

when I stood by her bed on Sundays,
so proud in my soap-smelling
special frock, and say *Ah,*
Bless your little cotton socks!

EMILY DICKINSON

He fumbles at your Soul
As Players at the Keys
Before they drop full Music on –
He stuns you by degrees –
Prepares your brittle Nature
For the Ethereal Blow
By fainter Hammers – further heard –
Then nearer – Then so slow
Your Breath has time to straighten –
Your Brain – to bubble Cool –
Deals – One – imperial – Thunderbolt –
That scalps your naked Soul –

When Winds take Forests in their Paws –
The Universe – is still –

THOMAS CAREW

The Compliment

My dearest, I shall grieve thee
When I swear, yet sweet believe me,
By thine eyes – the tempting book
On which even crabbed old men look –
I swear to thee (though none abhor them)
Yet I do not love thee for them.

I do not love thee for that fair
Rich fan of thy most curious hair,
Though the wires thereof be drawn
Finer than the threads of lawn
And are softer than the leaves
On which the subtle spinner weaves.

I do not love thee for those flowers
Growing on thy cheeks (love's bowers),
Though such cunning them hath spread
None can part their white and red;
Love's golden arrows thence are shot,
Yet for them I love thee not.

I do not love thee for those soft
Red coral lips I've kissed so oft,
Nor teeth of pearl, the double guard
To speech, whence music still is heard –
Though from those lips a kiss being taken
Might tyrants melt and death awaken.

I do not love thee (O my fairest)
For that richest, for that rarest
Silver pillar which stands under
Thy round head, that globe of wonder,
Though that neck be whiter far
Than towers of polished ivory are.

I do not love thee for those mountains
Hilled with snow, whence milky fountains
(Sugared sweet, as syrup'd berries)
Must one day run through pipes of cherries;
O how much those breasts do move me –
Yet for them I do not love thee.

I do not love thee for that belly,
Sleek as satin, soft as jelly,
Though within that crystal round
Heaps of treasure might be found
So rich that for the least of them
A king might leave his diadem.

I do not love thee for those thighs
Whose alabaster rocks do rise
So high and even that they stand
Like sea-marks to some happy land.
Happy are those eyes have seen them;
More happy they that sail between them.

I love thee not for thy moist palm
Though the dew thereof be balm,
Nor for thy pretty leg and foot,
Although it be the precious root
On which this goodly cedar grows;
Sweet, I love thee not for those,

Nor for thy wit, though pure and quick,
Whose substance no arithmetic
Can number down; nor for those charms
Masked in thy embracing arms –
Though in them one night to lie,
Dearest, I would gladly die.

I love not for those eyes, nor hair,
Nor cheeks, nor lips, nor teeth so rare,
Nor for thy speech, thy neck, or breast,
Nor for thy belly, nor the rest,
Nor for thy hand nor foot so small –
But, wouldst thou know, dear sweet – for all.

GAVIN EWART

Pantoum: Worship

So much I deify your glorious globes
(and kiss your round re-entrants and your cleft –
the Oriental earrings in your lobes
are all you wear) I touch both right and left

and kiss. Your round re-entrants and your cleft!
On your white skin the blacks of body hair
are all you wear (I touch). Both right and left
I see a Heaven feminine and fair,

on your white skin the blacks of body hair,
where both shine with a single, sexual light,
I see a Heaven feminine and fair
that overwhelms me now – it is so bright

where both shine with a single, sexual light,
the two, the privileged, that make the love!
That overwhelms me. Now, it is so bright –
yet comforting, the finger in the glove,

the two, the privileged, that make the love
(the Oriental earrings in your lobes),
yet comforting (the finger in the glove).
So much I deify your glorious globes!

WALT WHITMAN

We Two Boys Together Clinging

We two boys together clinging,
One the other never leaving,
Up and down the roads going, North and South
    excursions making,
Power enjoying, elbows stretching, fingers clutching,
Arm'd and fearless, eating, drinking, sleeping, loving,
No law less than ourselves owning, sailing, soldiering,
    thieving, threatening,
Misers, menials, priests alarming, air breathing, water
    drinking, on the turf or the sea-beach dancing,
Cities wrenching, ease scorning, statutes mocking,
    feebleness chasing,
Fulfilling our foray.

SIR CHARLES SEDLEY

On the Happy Corydon and Phyllis

Young Corydon and Phyllis
  Sat in a lovely grove,
Contriving crowns of lilies,
  Repeating toys of love,
And something else, but what I dare not name.

But as they were a-playing,
  She ogled so the swain;
It saved her plainly saying
  Let's kiss to ease our pain:
And something else, but what I dare not name.

A thousand times he kissed her,
  Laying her on the green;
But as he farther pressed her,
  A pretty leg was seen:
And something else, but what I dare not name.

So many beauties viewing,
  His ardour still increased;
And greater joys pursuing,
  He wandered o'er her breast:
And something else, but what I dare not name.

A last effort she trying,
  His passion to withstand;
Cried, but it was faintly crying,
  Pray take away your hand:
And something else, but what I dare not name.

Young Corydon grown bolder,
    The minutes would improve;
This is the time, he told her,
    To show you how I love;
And something else, but what I dare not name.

The nymph seemed almost dying,
    Dissolved in amorous heat;
She kissed and told him sighing,
    My dear your love is great:
And something else, but what I dare not name.

But Phyllis did recover
    Much sooner than the swain;
She blushing asked her lover,
    Shall we not kiss again:
And something else, but what I dare not name.

Thus Love his revels keeping,
    'Til Nature at a stand;
From talk they fell to sleeping,
    Holding each others hand;
And something else, but what I dare not name.

E. E. CUMMINGS

may I feel said he

may i feel said he
(i'll squeal said she
just once said he)
it's fun said she

(may i touch said he
how much said she
a lot said he)
why not said she

(let's go said he
not too far said she
what's too far said he
where you are said she)

may i stay said he
(which way said she
like this said he
if you kiss said she

may i move said he
is it love said she)
if you're willing said he
(but you're killing said she

but it's life said he
but your wife said she
now said he)
ow said she

(tiptop said he
don't stop said she
oh no said he)
go slow said she

(cccome? said he
ummm said she)
you're divine! said he
(you are Mine said she)

GRACE NICHOLS

My Black Triangle

My black triangle
sandwiched
between the geography
of my thighs

is a bermuda
of tiny atoms
forever seizing
and releasing
the world

My black triangle
is so rich
that it flows over
on to the dry crotch
of the world

My black triangle
is black light
sitting on the threshold
of the world

overlooking my deep-pink
probabilities

and though
it spares a thought
for history
my black triangle
has spread beyond history
beyond the dry fears of parch-ri-archy

spreading and growing
trusting and flowing
my black triangle
carries the seal of approval
of my deepest self

ROBERT HERRICK

Fresh Cheese and Cream

Wo'd yee have fresh Cheese and Cream?
Julia's Breast can give you them:
And if more; Each *Nipple* cries,
To your *Cream*, here's *Strawberries*.

D. H. LAWRENCE

Figs

The proper way to eat a fig, in society,
Is to split it in four, holding it by the stump,
And open it, so that it is a glittering, rosy, moist, honied,
    heavy-petalled four-petalled flower.

Then you throw away the skin
Which is just like a four-petalled calyx,
After you have taken off the blossom with your lips.

But the vulgar way
Is just to put your mouth to the crack, and take out the
    flesh in one bite.

Every fruit has its secret.

The fig is a very secretive fruit.
As you see it standing growing, you feel at once it is
    symbolic:
And it seems male.
But when you come to know it better, you agree with the
    Romans, it is female.

The Italians vulgarly say, it stands for the female part; the
    fig-fruit:
The fissure, the yoni,
The wonderful moist conductivity towards the centre.

Involved,
Inturned,
The flowering all inward and womb-fibrilled;
And but one orifice.

The fig, the horse-show, the squash-blossom.
Symbols.

There was a flower that flowered inward, womb-ward;
Now there is a fruit like a ripe womb.
It was always a secret.
That's how it should be, the female should always be
    secret.

There never was any standing aloft and unfolded on a
    bough
Like other flowers, in a revelation of petals;
Silver-pink peach, venetian glass of medlars and sorb-apples,
Shallow wine-cups on short, bulging stems
Openly pledging heaven:
Here's to the thorn in flower! Here is to Utterance!
The brave, adventurous rosaceae.

Folded upon itself, and secret unutterable,
And milk-sapped, sap that curdles milk and makes *ricotta*,
Sap that smells strange on your fingers, that even goats
    won't taste it;
Folded upon itself, enclosed like any Mohammedan
    woman,
Its nakedness all within-walls, its flowering forever unseen,
One small way of access only, and this close-curtained
    from the light;
Fig, fruit of the female mystery, covert and inward,
Mediterranean fruit, with your covert nakedness,
Where everything happens invisible, flowering and
    fertilisation, and fruiting
In the inwardness of your you, that eye will never see
Till it's finished, and you're over-ripe, and you burst to
    give up your ghost.

Till the drop of ripeness exudes,
And the year is over.

That's how the fig dies, showing her crimson through the
   purple slit
Like a wound, the exposure of her secret, on the open day.
Like a prostitute, the bursten fig, making a show of her
   secret.

That's how women die too.

The year is fallen over-ripe,
The year of our women.
The year of our women is fallen over-ripe.
The secret is laid bare.
And rottenness soon sets in.
The year of our women is fallen over-ripe.

When Eve once knew *in her mind* that she was naked
She quickly sewed fig-leaves, and sewed the same for the
   man.
She'd been naked all her days before,
But till then, till that apple of knowledge, she hadn't had
   the fact on her mind.

She got the fact on her mind, and quickly sewed fig-leaves.
And women have been sewing ever since.
But now they stitch to adorn the bursten fig, not to cover
   it.
They have their nakedness more than ever on their mind,
And they won't let us forget it.

Now, the secret
Becomes an affirmation through moist, scarlet lips
That laugh at the Lord's indignation.

What then, good Lord! cry the women.
We have kept our secret long enough.
We are a ripe fig.
Let us burst into affirmation.

They forget, ripe figs won't keep.
Ripe figs won't keep.

Honey-white figs of the north, black figs with scarlet
    inside, of the south.
Ripe figs won't keep, won't keep in any clime.
What then, when women the world over have all bursten
    into self-assertion?
And bursten figs won't keep?

ROBERT HERRICK

The Vine

I dreamed this mortal part of mine
Was metamorphosed to a vine;
Which crawling one and every way,
Enthralled my dainty Lucia.
Me thought, her long small legs and thighs
I with my tendrils did surprise;
Her belly, buttocks, and her waist
By now soft nervelets were embraced:
About her head I writhing hung,
And with rich clusters (hid among
The leaves) her temples I behung
So that my Lucia seemed to me
Young Bacchus ravished by his tree.
My curls about her neck did crawl,
And arms and hands they did enthral:
So that she could not freely stir,
(All parts there made one prisoner).
But when I crept with leaves to hide
Those parts, which maids keep unespied,
Such fleeting pleasures there I took,
That with the fancy I awoke;
And found (Ah me!) this flesh of mine
More like a stock, than like a vine.

SUJATA BHATT

Shérdi[1]

The way I learned
to eat sugar cane in Sanosra:
I use my teeth
to tear the outer hard *chaal*
then, bite off strips
of the white fibrous heart –
suck hard with my teeth, press down
and the juice spills out.

January mornings
the farmer cuts tender green sugar-cane
and brings it to our door.
Afternoons, when the elders are asleep
we sneak outside carrying the long smooth stalks.
The sun warms us, the dogs yawn,
our teeth grow strong
our jaws are numb;
for hours we suck out the *russ*, the juice sticky all over our hand.

So tonight
when you tell me to use my teeth,
to suck hard, harder,
then, I smell sugar cane grass
                    in your hair
and imagine you'd like to be
shérdi   shérdi   out in the fields
            the stalks sway
                    opening a path before us.

1 Sugar cane in Gujerati, the poet's first language.

64

C. P. CAVAFY *translated by Edmund Keeley and Philip Sherrard*

Two Young Men, 23 to 24 Years Old

He'd been sitting in the café since ten-thirty
expecting him to turn up any minute.
Midnight had gone, and he was still waiting for him.
It was now after one-thirty, and the café was almost
    deserted.
He'd grown tired of reading newspapers
mechanically. Of his three lonely shillings
only one was left: waiting that long,
he'd spent the others on coffees and brandy.
And he'd smoked all his cigarettes.
So much waiting had worn him out.
Because alone like that for so many hours,
he'd also begun to have disturbing thoughts
about the immoral life he was living.

But when he saw his friend come in –
weariness, boredom, thought all disappeared at once.

His friend brought unexpected news.
He'd won sixty pounds playing cards.

Their good looks, their exquisite youthfulness,
the sensitive love they shared
were refreshed, livened, invigorated
by the sixty pounds from the card table.

Now all joy and vitality, feeling and charm,
they went – not to the homes of their respectable families
(where they were no longer wanted anyway) –
they went to a familiar and very special
house of debauchery, and they asked for a bedroom
and expensive drinks, and they drank again.

And when the expensive drinks were finished
and it was close to four in the morning,
happy, they gave themselves to love.

JOHN DRYDEN

Song: from *An Evening's Love*

Calm was the Even, and clear was the sky
  And the new budding flowers did spring,
When all alone went Amyntas and I
  To hear the sweet Nightingale sing;
I sat, and he laid him down by me;
  But scarcely his breath he could draw;
For when with a fear he began to draw near,
  He was dash'd with A ha ha ha ha!

He blush'd to himself, and lay still for a while,
  And his modesty curb'd his desire;
But straight I convinc'd all his fear with a smile,
  Which added new flames to his fire.
'O Sylvia', he said, 'you are cruel,
  To keep your poor Lover in awe';
Then once more he pressed with his hand to my breast,
But was dash'd with A ha ha ha ha.

I knew 'twas his passion that caus'd all his fear;
  And therefore I pitied his case:
I whisper'd him softly 'There's no body near',
  And laid my cheek close to his face:
But as he grew bolder and bolder,
  A Shepherd came by us and saw;
And just as our bliss we began with a kiss,
  He laughed out with A ha ha ha ha.

PETER READING

Tryst

Me and Gib likes it here – always comes of a night,
no one else gets here, see. That's his Great-Grandad's stone.
Gassed, *he* was; got sent home from one of them *old* wars:
    Tommy, they called him.

We sprayed HARTLEPOOL WANKERS on one of them.
  Great!
This is the newest one – sad it is, really, it's
some little ten-year-old girlie's. Them plastic daffs
    look very nice, though.

He likes to get me down in the long weeds between
two of them marble things – I can see ivy sprout
on the cross by his head. He makes me squiggle when
    he sticks his hand up.

He works at one of them mills what makes cattle food.
He stacks the sacks. You should see them tattoos on his
arms when he flexes them. There is a big red heart
    with TRUE LOVE on it.

He runs the Packer-thing all on his own, he does.
We've saving up to get married and have a big
do like that big snob that works in our office had
    (Crystal, her name is).

I let him do what he wants – he pretends that he's
the Ripper, sometimes, and get me down on a grave;
then what he does with his hands feels like scurrying
    rats up my T-shirt.

When we're saved up enough, we're going to wed in church.
This is alright, though – at least in the summertime.
They don't pay poor Gib much, stacking them heavy sacks
    off the conveyor.

JOHN DONNE

The Ecstasy

Where, like a pillow on a bed,
    A pregnant bank swelled up, to rest
The violet's reclining head,
    Sat we two, one another's best.

Our hands were firmly cemented
    With a fast balm, which thence did spring;
Our eye-beams twisted, and did thread
    Our eyes upon one double string;

So to entergraft our hands, as yet
    Was all our means to make us one.
And pictures on our eyes to get
    Was all our propagation.

As 'twixt two equal armies, Fate
    Suspends uncertain victory,
Our souls (which to advance their state
    Were gone out) hung 'twixt her and me.

And whilst our souls negotiate there,
    We like sepulchral statues lay;
All day the same our postures were,
    And we said nothing all the day.

If any, so by love refined
    That he soul's language understood,
And by good love were grown all mind,
    Within convenient distance stood,

He (though he knew not which soul spake,
    Because both meant, both spake the same)
Might thence a new concoction take,
    And part far purer than he came.

This ecstasy doth unperplex
    (We said) and tell us what we love,
We see by this, it was not sex,
    We see, we saw not what did move:

But as all several souls contain
    Mixture of things, they know not what,
Love these mixed souls doth mix again,
    And makes both one, each this and that.

A single violet transplant,
    The strength, the colour, and the size,
(All which before was poor and scant)
    Redoubles still, and multiplies.

When love with one another so
    Interinanimates two souls,
That abler soul, which thence doth flow,
    Defects of loneliness controls.

We then, who are this new soul, know
    Of what we are composed, and made,
For the atomies of which we grow
    Are souls, whom no change can invade.

But, O alas! so long, so far
    Our bodies why do we forbear?
They are ours, though they are not we; we are
    The intelligences, they the sphere.

We owe them thanks, because they thus
    Did us, to us, at first convey,
Yielded their forces, sense, to us,
    Nor are dross to us, but allay.

On man heaven's influence works not so,
    But that it first imprints the air;
So soul into the soul may flow,
    Though it to body first repair.

As our blood labours to beget
    Spirits, as like souls as it can;
Because such fingers need to knit
    That subtle knot, which makes us man;

So must pure lovers' souls descend
    To affections, and to faculties,
Which sense may reach and apprehend,
    Else a great Prince in prison lies.

To our bodies turn we then, that so
    Weak men on love revealed may look;
Love's mysteries in souls do grow,
    But yet the body is his book.

And if some lover, such as we,
    Have heard this dialogue of one,
Let him still mark us, he shall see
    Small change, when we're to bodies gone.

PAUL VERLAINE *translated by Roland Grant and
Paul Archer*

Spring

Tender, the young auburn woman,
   By such innocence aroused,
Said to the blonde young girl
   These words, in a soft low voice:

'Sap which mounts, and flowers which thrust,
   Your childhood is a bower:
Let my fingers wander in the moss
   Where glows the rosebud.

'Let me among the clean grasses
   Drink the drops of dew
Which sprinkle the tender flower, –

'So that pleasure, my dear,
   Should brighten your open brow
Like dawn the reluctant blue.'

Her dear rare body, harmonious,
Fragrant, white as white
Rose, whiteness of pure milk, and rosy
As a lily beneath purple skies?

Beauteous thighs, upright breasts,
The back, the loins and belly, feast
For the eyes and prying hands
And for the lips and all the senses.

'Little one, let us see if your bed
Has still beneath the red curtain
The beautiful pillow that slips so
And the wild sheets. O to your bed!'

DO IT AGAIN

[I want you to know;]
I prayed that for us
                    the night
                              could last twice as long

SAPPHO *translated by Josephine Balmer*

SAPPHO *translated by Mary Barnard*

It was you, Atthis, who said

'Sappho, if you will not get
up and let us look at you
I shall never love you again!

'Get up, unleash your suppleness,
lift off your Chian nightdress
and, like a lily leaning into

'a spring, bathe in the water.
Cleis is bringing your best
purple frock and the yellow

'tunic down from the clothes chest;
you will have a cloak thrown over
you and flowers crowning your hair . . .

'Praxinoa, my child, will you please
roast nuts for our breakfast? One
of the gods is being good to us:

'today we are going at last
into Mitylene, our favourite
city, with Sappho, loveliest

'of its women; she will walk
among us like a mother with
all her daughters around her

'when she comes home from exile . . .'

But you forget everything . . .

PUBLIUS OVIDIUS NASO (OVID)
translated by Christopher Marlowe

In Summer's Heat

In summer's heat and mid-time of the day,
To rest my limbs upon a bed a lay,
One window shut, the other open stood,
Which gave such light as twinkles in a wood
Like twilight glimpse at setting of the sun,
Or night being past and yet not day begun.
Such light to shamefaced maidens must be shown,
Where they may sport, and seem to be unknown.
Then came Corinna in a long, loose gown,
Her white neck hid with tresses hanging down,
Resembling fair Semiramis going to bed,
Or Lais of a thousand wooers sped.
I snatched her gown, being thin the harm was small,
Yet strived she to be covered therewithal,
And, striving thus as one that would be chaste,
Betrayed herself, and yielded at the last.
Stark naked as she stood before mine eye,
Not one wen in her body could I spy.
What arms and shoulders did I touch and see?
How apt her breasts were to be pressed by me?
How smooth a belly under her waist saw I?
How large a leg, and what a lusty thigh?
To leave the rest, all liked me passing well;
I clinged her naked body, down she fell.
Judge you the rest. Being tired, she bade me kiss.
Jove send me more such afternoons as this.

CRAIG RAINE

Sexual Couplets

Here we are, without our clothes,
one excited watering can, one peculiar rose . . .

My shoe-tree wants to come,
and stretch your body where it lies undone . . .

I am wearing a shiny sou'wester;
you are coxcombed like a jester . . .

Oh my strangely gutted one,
the fish head needs your flesh around its bone . . .

We move in anapaestic time and pause,
until my body rhymes with yours . . .

In the valley of your arse,
all flesh is grass, all flesh is grass . . .

One damp acorn on the tweedy sod –
then the broad bean dangles in its pod . . .

CATULLUS *translated by Rodney Pybus*

Dearest Ipsitilla

Dearest Ipsitilla, I'd absolutely love it,
my darling girl, my gorgeous smarty-pants –
do send for me to come . . . this afternoon.
And when you do, it would be very helpful if
you'd please ensure that no one's barred the way
to your front door, and you're *at home*: don't you
slip off! Stay put, and get things ready for
our feast of nine successive inter-courses!
You really want some action? Ask me *now*!
I'm stuffed with breakfast, all stretched out, and you
should see my banger blasting through the sheets!

SAPPHO *translated by Josephine Balmer*

You've come and you –

                oh, I was longing for you –

have cooled my heart

                which was burning with desire

LIZ LOCHHEAD

Sexual Etiquette

Sexual etiquette,
Sexual etiquette
How to get more of it
And get more out of what you get.

I wonder if you realize
How across this once proud nation
Night-in night-out
There's thousands of women on the receiving end
Of premature ejaculation.

See there's women knowing what they want
But being too shy to mention
So that what ought to be
A fountain of joy
Is more a bone of contention.

Sexual etiquette,
Sexual etiquette
How to get more of it
And get more out of what you get.

How to ask – very nicely –
Yet sufficiently precisely.

If your husband tends to kiss you
As if you were his auntie,
If he thinks that a clitoris
Is a flowering potted plant, he
And I let my oaxters grow back in
Really rid and thick and hairy.

Because the theory of feminism's aw very well
But yiv got tae see it fur yirsel
Every individual hus tae realize
Her hale fortune isnae in men's eyes,
Say enough is enough
Away and get stuffed.

MAXIMIANUS ETRUSCUS (MAXIMIAN)

from *Elegies of Old Age*

Elegy V

   I wish't, I ask't, and gain'd the Beautious She;
But, oh! what Witchcraft did Enervate me!
Lifeless I on that mass of Beauty lay,
Nor the due debts of Sacred Love could pay.
All vigorous warmth my languid Limbs forsook,
And left me cold, like an old sapless Oak.
My chief, yet basest Nerve, did then prove lank,
And, like a Coward, from the Battle shrank;
Shrivell'd, and dry, like a dead wither'd flow'r,
Depriv'd, and void of all vivisick pow'r.
No fertile Moisture, no prolifick Juice,
Could the enfeebled Instrument produce;
No unctious Substance, no kind Balm emit;
Balm, nourishing as Milk, as Honey sweet
At last cry'd out the Disappointed Fair,
Thy dull unactive weight I cannot bear;
Thy heavy Limbs press me with joyless pain,
And all thy faint Endeavours are in vain.
   Useless, I must confess, I then did lye,
O'er-come of Thuscan grave Simplicitie;
And in soft Græcian Dalliance unskill'd,
To Age's Impotence was forc'd to yield.
Those very Arts, those Stratagems of Love,
(Which did, of old, Troy's sad Destruction prove,
And, maugre Hector's Courage, could prevail,)
Us'd to one Old defective Man, did fail:
Nay, though a Beauty, ev'n as Hellen bright,

Did to the mighty Task of Love invite.
Yet in the vain performance did I tire,
Though giv'n up to th' Empire of Desire.
Nor need I blush to own, or be asham'd;
That I by such a Beauty was inflam'd;
For Jove himself, had he my Goddess seen,
Ev'n Jove himself her Captive must have been.
Yet ne'ertheless, such was my first sad Night,
That I could neither give nor take Delight.
But a base conscious shame possest each sence,
Nor left me pow'r to make the least defence,
Dash'd with the Guilt of my own Impotence.

PHILODEMOS OF GADARA *translated by*
Fiona Pitt-Kethley

from *The Greek Anthology*

Charito's sixty now, her curly hair
Is still as black as it once was, her breasts,
Like marble cones, uplift without a bra.
Ambrosia distils from her firm flesh,
A thousand graces, everything that stirs . . .
You lovers who don't shrink from red-hot passion,
Roll up, and never mind the lady's years.

PATRICK O'SHAUGHNESSY

Endpiece

Here lies the body of Patrick
Who served Aphrodite delightedly.
Even when quite geriatric
He still raised a nightie excitedly.

THOM GUNN

Lines for My 55th Birthday

The love of old men is not worth a lot,
Desperate and dry even when it is hot.
You cannot tell what is enthusiasm
And what involuntary clawing spasm.

ANON

Stand, Stately Tavie

Stand, stately Tavie, out of the codpiece rise,
And dig a grave between thy mistress' thighs;
Swift stand, then stab 'till she replies,
Then gently weep, and after weeping, die.
Stand, Tavie, and gain thy credit lost;
Or by this hand I'll never draw thee, but against a post.

THOMAS HEYWOOD

She that Denies Me

She that denies me, I would have;
  Who craves me, I despise:
Venus hath power to rule mine heart,
  But not to please mine eyes.
Temptations offered, I still scorn,
  Denied, I cling them still;
I'll neither glut mine appetite
  Nor seek to starve my will.

Diana, double-clothed, offends –
  So Venus, naked quite.
The last begets a surfeit, and
  The other no delight.
That crafty girl shall please me best
  That 'no' for 'yea' can say,
And every wanton willing kiss
  Can season with a 'nay'.

HOMER *translated by William Congreve*

from the *Homeric Hymn to Venus*

Venus and Anchises

*Here, Venus pretends to be an ordinary woman to put
  'the panting youth' at his ease.*

Resistless love invading thus his breast,
The panting youth the smiling queen addrest.
'Since mortal you, of mortal mother came,
And Otreus you report your father's name,
And since the immortal Hermes from above,
To execute the dread commands of Jove,
Your wondrous beauties hither has convey'd,
A nuptial life with me henceforth to lead;
This instant will I seize upon thy charms,
Mix with thy soul, and melt within thy arms:
Tho' Phoebus, arm'd with his unerring dart,
Stood ready to transfix my panting heart;
Tho' death, tho' hell, in consequence attend,
Thou shalt with me the genial bed ascend.'
He said, and sudden snatch'd her beauteous hand;
The goddess smil'd, nor did th'attempt withstand,
But fix'd her eyes upon the hero's bed,
Where soft and silken coverlets were spread,
And over all a counterpane was plac'd,
Thick sown with furs of many a savage beast,
Of bears and lions, heretofore his spoil,
And still remain'd the trophies of his toil.
  Now to ascend the bed they both prepare,
And he with eager haste disrobes the fair.

Her sparkling necklace first he laid aside,
Her bracelets next, and braided hair unty'd;
And now his busy hand her zone unbrac'd,
Which girt her radiant robe about her waist;
Her radiant robe at last aside was thrown,
Whose rosy hue with dazzling lustre shone.
   The Queen of Love the youth thus disarray'd,
And on a chair of gold her vestments laid.
Anchises now (so Jove and Fate ordain'd)
The sweet extreme of ecstasy attain'd;
And mortal he was like th'immortals bless'd,
Not conscious of the goddess he possess'd.

EZRA POUND

Night Song

And have you thoroughly kissed my lips?
   There was no particular haste,
And are you not ready when evening's come?
   There's no *particular* haste.

You've got the whole night before you,
   Heart's-all-beloved-my-own;
In an uninterrupted night one can
   Get a good deal of kissing done.

JOHN DONNE

To His Mistress Going to Bed

Come, Madam, come, all rest my powers defy,
Until I labour, I in labour lie.
The foe oft-times having the foe in sight,
Is tired with standing though they never fight.
Off with that girdle, like heaven's zone glistering,
But a far fairer world encompassing.
Unpin that 'spangled' breastplate which you wear,
That th' eyes of busy fools may be stopped there.
Unlace yourself, for that harmonious chime
Tells me from you, that now 'tis your bed time.
Off with that happy busk, which I envy,
That still can be, and still can stand so nigh.
Your gown going off, such beauteous state reveals,
As when from flowery meads th' hill's shadow steals.
Off with that wiry coronet and show
The hairy diadem which on you doth grow;
Now off with those shoes, and then safely tread
In this love's hallowed temple, this soft bed.
In such white robes heaven's angels used to be
Received by men; thou angel bring'st with thee
A heaven like Mahomet's paradise; and though
Ill spirits walk in white, we easily know
By this these angels from an evil sprite,
Those set our hairs, but these our flesh upright.
    Licence my roving hands, and let them go
Before, behind, between, above, below.
O my America, my new found land,
My kingdom, safeliest when with one man manned,
My mine of precious stones, my empery,

How blessed am I in this discovering thee!
To enter in these bonds, is to be free;
Then where my hand is set, my seal shall be.
    Full nakedness, all joys are due to thee.
As souls unbodied, bodies unclothed must be,
To taste whole joys. Gems which you women use
Are like Atlanta's balls, cast in men's views,
That when a fool's eye lighteth on a gem,
His earthly soul may covet theirs, not them.
Like pictures, or like books' gay coverings made
For laymen, are all women thus arrayed;
Themselves are mystic books, which only we
Whom their imputed grace will dignify
Must see revealed. Then since I may know,
As liberally, as to a midwife, show
Thyself: cast all, yea, this white linen hence,
Here is no penance, much less innocence.
    To teach thee, I am naked first, why then
What needst thou have more covering than a man.

THOM GUNN

Philemon and Baucis

love without shadows – W.C.W.

Two trunks like bodies, bodies like twined trunks
Supported by their wooden hug. Leaves shine
In tender habit at the extremities.
Truly each other's, they have embraced so long
Their barks have met and wedded in one flow
Blanketing both. Time lights the handsome bulk.
   The gods were grateful, and for comfort given
Gave comfort multiplied a thousandfold.
Therefore the couple leached into that soil
The differences prolonged through their late vigour
That kept their exchanges salty and abrasive,
And found, with loves balancing equally,
Full peace of mind. They put unease behind them
A long time back, a long time back forgot
How each woke separate through the pale grey night,
A long time back forgot the days when each
– Riding the other's nervous exuberance –
Knew the slow thrill of learning how to love
What, gradually revealed, becomes itself,
Expands, unsheathes, as the keen rays explore:
Invented in the continuous revelation.

They have drifted into a perpetual nap,
The peace of trees that all night whisper nothings.

ARTHUR SYMONS

White Heliotrope

The feverish room and that white bed,
The tumbled skirts upon a chair,
The novel flung half-open, where
Hat, hair-pins, puffs, and paints, are spread;

The mirror that has sucked your face
Into its secret deep of deeps,
And there mysteriously keeps
Forgotten memories of grace;

And you, half dressed and half awake,
Your slant eyes strangely watching me,
And I, who watch you drowsily,
With eyes that, having slept not, ache;

This (need one dread? nay, dare one hope?)
Will rise, a ghost of memory, if
Ever again my handkerchief
Is scented with White Heliotrope.

ROBERT HERRICK

Upon the Nipples of Julia's Breast

Have ye beheld (with much delight)
A red rose peeping through a white?
Or else a cherry, double graced,
Within a lily-centre placed?
Or even marked the pretty beam
A strawberry shows half drowned in cream?

Or seen rich rubies blushing through
A pure, smooth pearl, and orient too?
So like to this, nay all the rest,
Is each sweet niplet of her breast.

GERARD MANLEY HOPKINS

Harry Ploughman

Hard as hurdle arms, with a broth of goldish flue
Breathed round; the rack of ribs; the scooped flank; lank
Rope-over thigh; knee-nave; and barrelled shank –
      Head and foot, shoulder and shank –
By a grey eye's heed steered well, one crew, fall to;
Stand at stress. Each limb's barrowy brawn, his thew
That onewhere curded, onewhere sucked or sank –
      Soared or sank –,
Though as a beechbole firm, finds his, as at a roll-call, rank
And features, in flesh, what deed he each must do –
      His sinew-service where do.

He leans to it, Harry bends, look. Back, elbow, and liquid
   waist
In him, all quail to the wallowing o' the plough: 's cheek
   crimsons; curls
Wag or crossbridle, in a wind lifted, windlaced –
      See his wind- lilylocks -laced;
Churlsgrace, too, child of Amansstrength, how it hangs or
   hurls
Them – broad in bluffhide his frowning feet lashed! raced
With, along them, cragiron under and cold furls –
      With-a-fountain's shining-shot furls.

TED HUGHES

Bride and Groom Lie Hidden for Three Days

She gives him his eyes, she found them
Among some rubble, among some beetles

He gives her her skin
He just seemed to pull it down out of the air and lay it
over her
She weeps with fearfulness and astonishment

She has found his hands for him, and fitted them freshly at
the wrists
They are amazed at themselves, they go feeling all over her

He has assembled her spine, he cleaned each piece carefully
And sets them in perfect order
A superhuman puzzle but he is inspired
She leans back twisting this way and that, using it and
laughing, incredulous

Now she has brought his feet, she is connecting them
So that his whole body lights up

And he has fashioned her new hips
With all fittings complete and with newly wound coils, all
shiningly oiled
He is polishing every part, he himself can hardly believe it

They keep taking each other to the sun, they find they can
easily
To test each new thing at each new step

And now she smooths over him the plates of his skull
So that the joints are invisible
And now he connects her throat, her breasts and the pit of
    her stomach
With a single wire

She gives him his teeth, tying their roots to the centrepin of
    his body

He sets the little circlets on her fingertips

She stitches his body here and there with steely purple silk

He oils the delicate cogs of her mouth

She inlays with deep-cut scrolls the nape of his neck

He sinks into place the inside of her thighs

So, gasping with joy, with cries of wonderment
Like two gods of mud
Sprawling in the dirt, but with infinite care

They bring each other to perfection.

PETER READING

Carte Postale

Dear Mum and Dad.
                    The picture shows a 'gendarme'
which means policeman. France is overrated.
For two weeks it has been wet. 9th September:
We had a 'dégustation' in the Côte
de Mâçonnais and Mal got quite light-headed.
Sometimes I think it will be *too* ideal
living with Mal – it's certainly the Real
Thing. I must go now – here comes Mal.
                                    Love, Crystal.

Encircling her slim waist with a fond arm,
the husband of a fortnight nibbles her throat,
would be dismayed to know how she had hated
that first night when in Calais he had kissed all
over her, and oh God!, how she now dreaded
each night the importunate mauve-capped swollen member.

W. B. YEATS

Leda and the Swan

A sudden blow; the great wings beating still
Above the staggering girl, her thighs caressed
By the dark webs, her nape caught in his bill,
He holds her helpless breast upon his breast.

How can those terrified vague fingers push
The feathered glory from her loosening thighs?
And how can body, laid in that white rush,
But feel the strange heart beating where it lies?

A shudder in the loins engenders there
The broken wall, the burning roof and tower
And Agamemnon dead.
                        Being so caught up,
So mastered by the brute blood of the air,
Did she put on his knowledge with his power
Before the indifferent beak could let her drop?

SEAMUS HEANEY

Rite of Spring

So winter closed its fist
And got it stuck in the pump.
The plunger froze up a lump

In its throat, ice founding itself
Upon iron. The handle
Paralysed at an angle.

Then the twisting of wheat straw
Into ropes, lapping them tight
Round stem and snout, then a light

That sent the pump up in flame.
It cooled, we lifted her latch,
Her entrance was wet, and she came.

ALISON FELL

In Confidence

(for the Writers' Group)

– An orgasm is like an anchovy,
she says,
little, long, and very salty.

– No, it's a caterpillar,
undulating, fat and sweet.

– A sunburst, says the third,
an exploding watermelon:
I had one at Christmas.

– Your body betrays, she says,
one way or another.
Rash and wriggling, it comes
and comes, while your mind
says lie low, or go.

– Or else it snarls and shrinks
to the corner of its cage

while your mind, consenting,
whips it on and out,
out in the open
and *so* free.

– As for me,
says the last,
if I have them brazen
with birthday candles,
with water faucets
or the handles of Toby Jugs,
I don't care who knows it.
But how few I have –
keep *that* in the dark.

E. E. CUMMINGS

from the *Collected Poems*

she being Brand

-new; and you
know consequently a
little stiff i was
careful of her and(having

thoroughly oiled the universal
joint tested my gas felt of
her radiator made sure her springs were O.

K.)i went right to it flooded-the-carburetor cranked her

up, slipped the
clutch(and then somehow got into reverse she
kicked what
the hell)next
minute i was back in neutral tried and

again slo-wly; bare,ly nudg. ing(my
lev-er Right-
oh and her gears being in
A 1 shape passed
from low through
second-in-to-high like
greasedlightning)just as we turned the corner of Divinity

avenue i touched the accelerator and give

her the juice, good
                    (it

was the first ride and believe i we was
happy to see how nice she acted right up to
the last minute coming back down by the Public
Gardens i slammed on

the
internalexpanding
&
externalcontracting
brakes Bothatonce and

brought allofher tremB
-ling
to a:dead.

stand-
;Still).

ALGERNON CHARLES SWINBURNE

Love and Sleep

Lying asleep between the strokes of night
   I saw my love lean over my sad bed,
   Pale as the duskiest lily's leaf or head,
Smooth-skinned and dark, with bare throat made to bite,

Too wan for blushing and too warm for white,
   But perfect-coloured without white or red,
   And her lips opened amorously, and said –
I wist not what, saving one word – Delight.
And all her face was honey to my mouth,
   And all her body pasture to mine eyes;
     The long lithe arms and hotter hands than fire,
The quivering flanks, hair smelling of the south,
   The bright light feet, the splendid supple thighs
     And glittering eyelids of my soul's desire.

THE SEVEN YEAR ITCH

I don't know what to do –
                              I'm torn in two

SAPPHO *translated by Josephine Balmer*

BEN JONSON

Song: to Celia

Come, my Celia, let us prove
While we may, the sports of love.
Time will not be ours for ever:
He at length our good will sever.
Spend not then his gifts in vain.
Suns that set may rise again,
But if once we lose this light
'Tis with us perpetual night.
Why should we defer our joys?
Fame and rumour are but toys.
Cannot we delude the eyes
Of a few poor household spies?
Or his easier ears beguile
So removed by our wile?
'Tis no sin love's fruit to steal,
But the sweet theft to reveal –
To be taken, to be seen –
These have crimes accounted been.

GRACE NICHOLS

The Decision

In restaurants he fed her
In bed said how he loved her
but she decided to leave him
because he was squeamish

Now she has a new lover
who doesn't feed her
or tell her he loves her
but who buries his face
in plain curiosity of her taste

And tells her how good she is O
And tells her how good she is.

CAROL ANN DUFFY

Oppenheim's Cup and Saucer

She asked me to luncheon in fur. Far from
the loud laughter of men, our secret life stirred.

I remember her eyes, the slim rope of her spine.
This is your cup, she whispered, and this mine.

We drank the sweet hot liquid and talked dirty.
As she undressed me, her breasts were a mirror

and there were mirrors in the bed. She said Place
your legs around my neck, that's right. Yes.

STEVIE SMITH

Infelice

Walking swiftly with a dreadful duchess,
He smiled too briefly, his face was as pale as sand,
He jumped into a taxi when he saw me coming,
Leaving me along with a private meaning,
He loves me so much, my heart is singing.
Later at the Club when I rang him in the evening
They said: Sir Rat is dining, is dining, is dining,
No Madam, he left no message, ah how his silence speaks
He loves me too much for words, my heart is singing.
The Pullman seats are here, the tickets for Paris, I am
    waiting.
Presently the telephone rings, it is his valet speaking,
Sir Rat is called away, to Scotland, his constituents,
(Ah the dreadful duchess, but he loves me best)
Best pleasure to the last, my heart is singing.
One night he came, it was four in the morning,
Walking slowly upstairs, he stands beside my bed,
Dear darling, lie beside me, it is too cold to stand speaking
He lies down beside me, his face is like the sand,
He is in a sleep of love, my heart is singing.
Sleeping softly softly, in the morning I must wake him,
And waking he murmurs, I only came to sleep.
The words are so sweetly cruel, how deeply he loves me,
I say them to myself alone, my heart is singing.
Now the sunshine strengthens, it is ten in the morning,
He is so timid in love, he only needs to know,
He is my little child, how can he come if I do not call him,
I will write and tell him everything, I take the pen and write
I love you so much, my heart is singing.

LIZ LOCHHEAD

After Leaving the Castle

On the first night
the lady lay in the dark with her lover
awake all night
afraid her husband would pursue her.

On the second night
the lady lay awake in the arms of her lover
her tongue and teeth idly
exploring the cold of his earring.

On the third night
the lady lay awake afraid
her husband would never come after.

On the fourth night
the lady thought as she drifted off to sleep
how monotonous it was going to be
to live on rabbit stew forever
& she turned a little away
from snoring, the smell of wild garlic.

When they passed him on the road
on the fifth day,
she began to make eyes at the merchant.

RICHARD JONES

Wan Chu's Wife in Bed

Wan Chu, my adoring husband,
has returned from another trip
selling trinkets in the provinces.
He pulls off his lavender shirt
as I lay naked in our bed,
waiting for him. He tells me
I am the only woman he'll ever love.
He may wander from one side of China
to the other, but his heart
will always stay with me.
His face glows in the lamplight
with the sincerity of a boy
when I lower the satin sheet
to let him see my breasts.
Outside, it begins to rain
on the cherry trees
he planted with our son,
and when he enters me with a sigh,
the storm begins in earnest,
shaking our little house.
Afterwards, I stroke his back
until he falls asleep.
I'd love to stay awake all night
listening to the rain,
but I should sleep, too.
Tomorrow Wan Chu will be
a hundred miles away
and I will be awake all night
in the arms of Wang Chen,
the tailor from Ming Pao,
the tiny village down river.

WALT WHITMAN

When I Heard at the Close of the Day

When I heard at the close of the day how my name had
    been receiv'd with plaudits in the capitol, still it was not
    a happy night for me that follow'd,
And else when I carous'd, or when my plans were
    accomplish'd, still I was not happy,
But the day when I rose at dawn from the bed of perfect
    health, refresh'd, singing, inhaling the ripe breath of
    autumn,
When I saw the full moon in the west grow pale and
    disappear in the morning light,
When I wander'd alone over the beach, and undressing
    bathed, laughing with the cool waters, and saw the sun
    rise,
And when I thought how my dear friend my lover was on
    his way coming, O then I was happy,
O then each breath tasted sweeter, and all that day my food
    nourish'd me more, and the beautiful day pass'd well,
And the next came with equal joy, and with the next at
    evening came my friend,
And that night while all was still I heard the waters roll
    slowly continually up the shores,
I heard the hissing rustle of the liquid and sands as
    directed to me whispering to congratulate me,
For the one I love most lay sleeping by me under the same
    cover in the cool night,
In the stillness in the autumn moonbeams his face was
    inclined toward me,
And his arm lay lightly around my breast – and that night
    I was happy.

The Husband Who Saw His Wife with Another Man

A peasant lay in wait inside
His house to see what could be spied.
He saw another man instead
Of him, enjoying his wife in bed.
'Alas,' he said, 'what have I seen?'
His wife replied: 'What do you mean?
Fair lord, my love, what did you see?'
'Another man, I'm sure,' said he,
'Was on the bed in your embrace.'
His wife, with anger in her face,
Replied, 'A man? Oh, very well,
You're sick again, that I can tell.
You cling to lies, as if they're true.'
'I trust my eyes – that I must do.'
'You're mad,' she said 'to think you can
Insist you saw me with a man.
Now tell the truth, at once, be good.'
'I saw him leaving for the wood.'
'Oh no!' she said, 'that means that I
Today or next day'll surely die.
It happened to my Gran, you see,
My mother too, and now to me.
It happened just before they died –
A fact well-known both far and wide.
A young man led both off, you know –
They had no other cause to go.
My end is near, the die is cast –

Send for my cousins, I need them fast.
Let's split up all our property –
I mustn't waste my time, you see.
With all the stuff that is my share,
I'll to a nunnery repair.'
The peasant heard, and cried in fear:
'Let be, let be, my sweetheart, dear,
Don't leave me now, like this, I pray –
I made up all I saw today.'
'I dare not stay, it's far too late –
I'm thinking of my spiritual state,
Especially, after the shame
That you've attached to my good name.
I will be blamed, I know I will
For treating you so very ill,
Unless, perhaps, you'd rather swear,
With all my family standing there,
You never saw a man with me.
You must swear also, don't you see?
This subject will be dropped and you
Will never nag me for it, too.'
He answered 'Lady, I agree.'
They both went off to church, and he
Soon swore to all she'd asked him for
All that, ah yes, and much much more.

   Take warning from this tale, men, do,
That women know a thing or two –
For strange deceits and knavish tricks,
Their talent's greater than Old Nick's.

GRACE NICHOLS

Grease

Grease steals in like a lover
over the body of my oven.
Grease kisses the knobs
of my stove.
Grease plays with the small
hands of my spoons.
Grease caresses the skin
of my table-cloth,
Getting into every crease.
Grease reassures me that life
is naturally sticky.

Grease is obviously having an affair with me.

ANON (*c.*1671)

Against Platonic Love

'Tis true, fair Celia, that by thee I live;
That every kiss, and every fond embrace
Forms a new soul within me, and doth give
A balsam to the wound made by thy face.
   Yet still methinks I miss
     That bliss
   Which lovers dare not name,
   And only then described is
   When flame doth meet with flame.

Those favours which do bless me every day
Are yet but empty and platonical.
Think not to please your servants with half pay.
Good gamesters never stick to throw at all.
   Who can endure to miss
     That bliss
   Which lovers dare not name,
   And only then described is
   When flame doth meet with flame?

If all those sweets within you must remain,
Unknown and ne'er enjoyed, like hidden treasure,
Nature, as well as I, will lose her name,
And you as well as I lose youthful pleasure.
   We wrong ourselves to miss
     That bliss
   Which lovers dare not name,
   And only then described is
   When flame doth meet with flame.

Our souls which long have peeped at one another
Out of the narrow casements of our eyes
Shall now by love conducted meet together
In secret caverns, where all pleasure lies.
   There, there we shall not miss
      That bliss
   Which lovers dare not name,
   And only then described is
   When flame doth meet with flame.

PUBLIUS OVIDIUS NASO (OVID)
translated by William Congreve

from the *Ars Amatoria (The Art of Love)*

Sometimes your lover to incite the more,
Pretend your husband's spies beset the door:
Tho' free as Thais, still affect a fright;
For seeming danger heightens the delight.
Oft' let the youth in thro' your window steal,
Tho' he might enter at the door as well;
And sometimes let your maid surprise pretend,
And beg you in some hole to hide your friend.
Yet ever and anon dispel his fear,
And let him taste of happiness sincere;
Lest, quite dishearten'd with too much fatigue,
He should grow weary of the dull intrigue.

But I forgot to tell how you may try
Both to evade the husband and the spy.

That wives should of their husbands stand in awe,
Agrees with justice, modesty, and law;
But that a mistress may be lawful prize,
None but her keeper I am sure denies.
For such fair nymphs these precepts are design'd,
Which ne'er can fail, join'd with a willing mind.
Tho' stuck with Argus' eyes your keeper were,
Advis'd by me you shall elude his care.

When you to wash or bathe retire from sight,
Can he observe what letters then you write?
Or can his caution against such provide,
Which in her breast your confidant may hide?
Can he that note beneath her garter view,
Or that which, more conceal'd, is in her shoe?

Yet these perceiv'd, you may her back undress,
And writing on her skin your mind express.
New milk, or pointed spires of flax, when green,
Will ink supply, and letters mark unseen;
Fair will the paper show, nor can be read
Till all the writings' with warm ashes spread.

Acrisus was with all his care betray'd,
And in his tow'r of brass a grandsire made.

Can spies avail when you to plays resort,
Or in the Circus view the noble sport?
Or can you be to Isis' fane pursu'd,
Or Cybelle's, whose rites all men exclude?
Tho' watchful servants to the bagnio come,
They're ne'er admitted to the bathing-room.
Or when some sudden sickness you pretend,
May you not take to your sick-bed a friend?
False keys a private passage may procure,
If not, there are more ways beside the door.
Sometimes with wine your watchful foll'wer treat;
When drunk you may with ease his care defeat;
Or, to prevent too sudden a surprise,
Prepare a sleeping draught to seal his eyes:
Or let your maid, still longer time to gain,
An inclination for his person feign:
With faint resistance let him drill him on,
And after competent delays be won.

But what need all these various doubtful wiles,
Since gold the greatest vigilance beguiles?
Believe me, men and gods with gifts are pleas'd,
Ev'n angry Jove with off'rings is appeas'd.
With presents fools and wise alike are caught;
Give but enough, the husband may be bought.
But let me warn you, when you bribe a spy,
That you for ever his connivance buy;

Pay him his price at once, for with such men
You'll know no end of giving now and then.
Once I remember, I with cause complain'd
Of jealousy, occasion'd by a friend.
Believe me, apprehensions of that kind
Are not alone to our false sex confin'd.
Trust not too far your she-companions truth,
Lest she sometimes should intercept the youth:
The very confidant that lends the bed
May entertain your lover in your stead.

GAVIN EWART

An Old Husband Suspects Adultery

I was just beginning to feel in the mood,
my desire was just beginning to harden,
as we lay cuddling like Babes in the Wood
or Adam and Eve naked in that Garden –
when the telephone started ringing.
She jumped out of bed (like Eve, naked)
and answered it – I could hear him darlinging.

She spoke to him coolly but she wasn't rude,
taking it in her stride with her long legs – flustered
she certainly wasn't. No thought of Bad or Good
grazed her. Domestic as custard
she talked, as if to a grocer,
like smooth-limbed Eve with a handset, naked,
standing there beautiful. I was feeling moroser

than I can tell you. A pin-up, a nude,
she'd made herself. Unreachable. She hung up
and climbed back into bed. Like Robin Hood
he'd robbed the rich – before he'd rung up
I'd really felt like doing it,
but now the thread was lost – Eve, so naked, couldn't
tempt me now into pursuing it.

KACCIPĒṬṬU NAṉṉĀKAIYĀR
translated by A. K. Ramanijan

My lover capable of terrible lies
at night lay close to me
in a dream
that lied like truth.

I woke up, still deceived,
and caressed the bed
thinking it my lover.

It's terrible. I grow lean
in loneliness,
like a water lily
gnawed by a beetle.

FEDERICO GARCÍA LORCA *translated by*
Stephen Spender and J. L. Gili

The Faithless Wife

So I took her to the river
believing she was a maiden,
but she already had a husband.

It was on Saint James's night
and almost as if I was obliged to.
The lanterns went out
and the crickets lighted up.
In the farthest street corners
I touched her sleeping breasts,
and they opened to me suddenly
like spikes of hyacinth.
The starch of her petticoat
sounded in my ears
like a piece of silk
rent by ten knives.
Without silver light on their foliage
the trees had grown larger
and a horizon of dogs
barked very far from the river.

Past the blackberries,
the reeds and the hawthorn,
underneath her cluster of hair
I made a hollow in the earth.
I took off my tie.
She took off her dress.
I my belt with the revolver.
She her four bodices.

Nor nard nor mother-o'-pearl
have skin so fine,
nor does glass with silver
shine with such brilliance.
Her thighs slipped away from me
like startled fish,
half full of fire,
half full of cold.
That night I ran
on the best of roads
mounted on a nacre mare
without bridle or stirrups.
As a man, I won't repeat
the things she said to me.
The light of understanding
has made me most discreet.
Smeared with sand and kisses
I took her away from the river.
The swords of the lilies
battled with the air.

I behaved like what I am.
Like a proper gipsy.
I gave her a large sewing basket,
of straw-coloured satin,
and I did not fall in love
for although she had a husband
she told me she was a maiden
when I took her to the river.

HUGO WILLIAMS

Prayer

God give me strength to lead a double life.
Cut me in half.
Make each half happy in its own way
with what is left. Let me disobey
my own best instincts
and do what I want to do, whatever that may be,
without regretting it, or thinking I might.

When I come home late at night from home,
saying I have to go away,
remind me to look out the window
to see which house I'm in.
Pin a smile on my face
when I turn up two weeks later with a tan
and presents for everyone.

Teach me how to stand and where to look
when I say the words
about where I've been
and what sort of time I've had.
Was it good or bad or somewhere in between?
I'd like to know how I feel about these things,
perhaps you'd let me know?

When it's time to go to bed in one of my lives,
go ahead of me up the stairs,
shine a light in the corners of my room.
Tell me this: do I wear pyjamas here,
or sleep with nothing on?
If you can't oblige by cutting me in half,
God give me strength to lead a double life.

C. P. CAVAFY *translated by Edmund Keeley and*
Philip Sherrard

One Night

The room was cheap and sordid,
hidden above the suspect taverna.
From the window you could see the alley,
dirty and narrow. From below
came the voices of workmen
playing cards, enjoying themselves.

And there on that ordinary, plain bed
I had love's body, knew those intoxicating lips,
red and sensual,
red lips so intoxicating
that now as I write, after so many years,
in my lonely house, I'm drunk with passion again.

CAROL ANN DUFFY

Adultery

Wear dark glasses in the rain
Regard what was unhurt
as though through a bruise.
Guilt. A sick, green tint.

New gloves, money tucked in the palms,
the handshake crackles. Hands
can do many things. Phone.
Open the wine. Wash themselves. Now

you are naked under your clothes all day,
slim with deceit. Only the once
brings you alone to your knees,
miming, more, more; older and sadder,

creative. Suck a lie with a hole in it
on the way home from a lethal, thrilling night
up against a wall, faster. Language
unpeels to a lost cry. You're a bastard.

Do it do it do it. Sweet darkness
in the afternoon: a voice in your ear
telling you how you are wanted,
which way, now. A telltale clock

wiping the hours from its face, your face
on a white sheet, gasping, radiant, yes.
Pay for it in cash, fiction, cab-fares back
to the life which crumbles like a wedding-cake.

Paranoia for lunch; too much
to drink, as a hand on your thigh
tilts the restaurant. You know all about love,
don't you. Turn on your beautiful eyes

for a stranger who's dynamite in bed, again
and again; a slow replay in the kitchen
where the slicing of innocent onions
scalds you to tears. Then, selfish autobiographical sleep

in a marital bed, the tarnished spoon of your body
stirring betrayal, your heart over-ripe at the core.
You're an expert, darling; your flowers
dumb and explicit on nobody's birthday.

So write the script – illness and debt,
a ring thrown away in a garden
no moon can heal, your own words
commuting to bile in your mouth, terror –

and all for the same thing twice. And all
for the same thing twice. You did it.
What. Didn't you. Fuck. Fuck. No. That was
the wrong verb. This is only an abstract noun.

ANNE SEXTON

For My Lover, Returning to His Wife

She is all there.
She was melted carefully down for you
and cast up from your childhood,
cast up from your one hundred favorite aggies.

She has always been there, my darling.
She is, in fact, exquisite.
Fireworks in the dull middle of February
and as real as a cast-iron pot.

Let's face it, I have been momentary.
A luxury. A bright red sloop in the harbor.
My hair rising like smoke from the car window.
Littleneck clams out of season.

She is more than that. She is your have to have,
has grown you your practical your tropical growth.
This is not an experiment. She is all harmony.
She sees to oars and oarlocks for the dinghy,

has placed wild flowers at the window at breakfast,
sat by the potter's wheel at midday,
set forth three children under the moon,
three cherubs drawn by Michelangelo,

done this with her legs spread out
in the terrible months in the chapel.
If you glance up, the children are there
like delicate balloons resting on the ceiling.

She has also carried each one down the hall
after supper, their heads privately bent,
two legs protesting, person to person,
her face flushed with a song and their little sleep.

I give you back your heart.
I give you permission —

for the fuse inside her, throbbing
angrily in the dirt, for the bitch in her
and the burying of her wound —
for the burying of her small red wound alive —

for the pale flickering flare under her ribs,
for the drunken sailor who waits in her left pulse,
for the mother's knee, for the stockings,
for the garter belt, for the call —

the curious call
when you will burrow in arms and breasts
and tug at the orange ribbon in her hair
and answer the call, the curious call.

She is so naked and singular.
She is the sum of yourself and your dream.
Climb her like a monument, step after step.
She is solid.

As for me, I am a watercolor.
I wash off.

GEORGE GORDON, LORD BYRON

When We Two Parted

When we two parted
   In silence and tears,
Half broken-hearted
   To sever for years,
Pale grew thy cheek and cold,
   Colder thy kiss;
Truly that hour foretold
   Sorrow to this.

The dew of the morning
   Sunk chill on my brow –
It felt like the warning
   Of what I feel now.
Thy vows are all broken,
   And light is thy fame:
I hear thy name spoken,
   And share in its shame.

They name thee before me,
   A knell to mine ear;
A shudder comes o'er me –
   Why wert thou so dear?
They know not I knew thee,
   Who knew thee too well: –
Long, long shall I rue thee,
   Too deeply to tell.

In secret we met –
　　In silence I grieve,
That thy heart could forget,
　　Thy spirit deceive.
If I should meet thee
　　After long years,
How should I greet thee?
　　With silence and tears.

JOHN AGARD

The Lover

What can i do

when he weaves
his spell
of softness
over you

what can i do

when his gentle
fingers touch
your eyes
like leaves

what can i do

when your cheeks
glow peace
and you weaken
in his presence

what can i do

when you open
to the lover
by the name
of sleep

NICHOLAS HOOKES

To Amanda Desirous to Go to Bed

Sleepy, my dear? yes, yes, I see
Morpheus is fallen in love with thee;
Morpheus, my worst of rivals, tries
To draw the curtains of thine eyes,
And fans them with his wing asleep;
Makes drowsy love to play bopeep.
How prettily his feathers blow
Those fleshy shuttings to and fro!
O how he makes me Tantalise
With those fair apples of thine eyes!
Eqivocates and cheats me still,
Opening and shutting at his will,
Now both, now one! the doting god
Plays with thine eyes at even or odd.
My stammering tongue doubts which it might
Bid thee, goodmorrow or goodnight.
So thy eyes twinkle brighter far
Than the bright trembling evening star;
So a wax taper burnt within
The socket, plays at out and in.
    Thus did Morpheus court thine eye,
Meaning there all night to lie:
Cupid and he play Whoop, All-Hid!
The eye, their bed and coverlid.
    Fairest, let me thy nightclothes air;
Come, I'll unlace thy stomacher.
Make me thy maiden chamberman,
Or let me be thy warming-pan.
O that I might but lay my head

At thy bed's feet i' th' trundle-bed.
Then i' th' morning ere I rose,
I'd kiss thy pretty pettitoes,
Those smaller feet with which i' th' day
My love so neatly trips away.
  Since you I must not wait upon,
Most modest lady, I'll be gone;
And though I cannot sleep with thee,
Oh may my dearest dream of me!
All the night long dream that we move
To the main centre of our love;
And if I chance to dream of thee,
Oh may I dream eternally!
Dream that we freely act and play
Those postures which we dream by day;
Spending our thoughts i' th' best delight
Chaste dreams allow of in the night.

I'M THROUGH WITH LOVE

The moon has set
                    and the stars have faded,
midnight has gone,
                    long hours pass by, pass by;
I sleep alone

SAPPHO *translated by Josephine Balmer*

C. P. CAVAFY *translated by Edmund Keeley and*
Philip Sherrard

Come Back

Come back often and take hold of me,
sensation that I love, come back and take hold of me –
when the body's memory revives
and an old longing again passes through the blood,
when lips and skin remember
and hands feel as though they touch again.

Come back often, take hold of me in the night
when lips and skin remember . . .

ERNEST DOWSON

Non Sum Qualis Eram Bonae Sub Regno Cynarae

Last night, ah, yesternight, betwixt her lips and mine
There fell thy shadow, Cynara! thy breath was shed
Upon my soul between the kisses and the wine;
And I was desolate and sick of an old passion,
   Yea, I was desolate and bowed my head:
I have been faithful to thee, Cynara! in my fashion.

All night upon mine heart I felt her warm heart beat,
Night-long within mine arms in love and sleep she lay;
Surely the kisses of her bought red mouth were sweet;
But I was desolate and sick of an old passion,
   When I awoke and found the dawn was grey:
I have been faithful to thee, Cynara! in my fashion.

I have forgot much, Cynara! gone with the wind,
Flung roses, roses riotously with the throng,
Dancing, to put thy pale, lost lilies out of mind;
But I was desolate and sick of an old passion,
   Yea, all the time, because the dance was long:
I have been faithful to thee, Cynara! in my fashion.

EDNA ST VINCENT MILLAY

What Lips My Lips Have Kissed

What lips my lips have kissed, and where, and why,
I have forgotten, and what arms have lain
Under my head till morning; but the rain
Is full of ghosts tonight, that tap and sigh
Upon the glass and listen for reply,
And in my heart there stirs a quiet pain
For unremembered lads that not again
Will turn to me at midnight with a cry.
Thus in the winter stands the lonely tree,
Nor knows what birds have vanished one by one,
Yet knows its boughs more silent than before:
I cannot say what loves have come and gone,
I only know that summer sang in me
A little while, that in me sings no more.

SIMON ARMITAGE

To His Lost Lover

Now they are no longer
any trouble to each other

he can turn things over, get down to that list
of things that never happened, all of the lost

unfinishable business.
For instance . . . for instance,

how he never clipped and kept her hair, or drew a hairbrush
through that style of hers, and never knew how not to blush

at the fall of her name in close company.
How they never slept like buried cutlery –

two spoons or forks cupped perfectly together,
or made the most of some heavy weather –

walked out into hard rain under sheet lightning,
or did the gears while the other was driving.

How he never raised his fingertips
to stop the segments of her lips

from breaking the news,
or tasted the fruit,

or picked for himself the pear of her heart,
or lifted her hand to where his own heart

was a small, dark, terrified bird
in her grip. Where it hurt.

Or said the right thing,
or put it in writing.

And never fled the black mile back to his house
before midnight, or coaxed another button of her blouse,

then another,
or knew her

favourite colour,
her taste, her flavour,

and never ran a bath or held a towel for her,
or soft-soaped her, or whipped her hair

into an ice-cream cornet or a beehive
of lather, or acted out of turn, or misbehaved

when he might have, or worked a comb
where no comb had been, or walked back home

through a black mile hugging a punctured heart,
where it hurt, where it hurt, or helped her hand

to his butterfly heart
in its two blue halves.

And never almost cried,
and never once described

an attack of the heart,
or under a silk shirt

nursed in his hand her breast,
her left, like a tear of flesh

wept by the heart,
where it hurts,

or brushed with his thumb the nut of her nipple,
or drank intoxicating liquors from her navel.

Or christened the Pole Star in her name,
or shielded the mask of her face like a flame,

a pilot light,
or stayed the night,

or steered her back to that house of his,
or said 'Don't ask me to say how it is

I like you.
I just might do.'

How he never figured out a fireproof plan,
or unravelled her hand, as if her hand

were a solid ball
of silver foil

and discovered a lifeline hiding inside it,
and measured the trace of his own alongside it.

But said some things and never meant them –
sweet nothings anybody could have mentioned.

And left unsaid some things he should have spoken,
about the heart, where it hurt exactly, and how often.

GEORGE GORDON, LORD BYRON

So, We'll Go No More a Roving

I

So, we'll go no more a roving
  So late into the night,
Though the heart be still as loving,
  And the moon be still as bright.

II

For the sword outwears its sheath,
  And the soul wears out the breast,
And the heart must pause to breathe,
  And love itself have rest.

III

Though the night was made for loving,
  And the day returns too soon,
Yet we'll go no more a roving
  By the light of the moon.

SEAMUS HEANEY

Victorian Guitar

for David Hammond

*Inscribed 'Belonged to Louisa Catherine Coe before
her marriage to John Charles Smith, March 1852.'*

I expected the lettering to carry
The date of the gift, a kind of christening:
This is more like the plate on a coffin.

Louisa Catherine Smith could not be light.
Far more than a maiden name
Was cancelled by him on the first night.

I believe he cannot have known your touch
Like this instrument – for clearly
John Charles did not hold with fingering –

Which is obviously a lady's:
The sound-box trim as a girl in stays,
The neck right for the smallest span.

Did you even keep track of it as a wife?
Do you know the man who has it now
Is giving it the time of its life?

JOAN VAN POZNAK

Viola d'Amore

'Woman is a delightful instrument, of which love is the bow, and man the artist.' Stendhal

She was his instrument, and oh,
How well he wielded love's bow.
At any hour, in any key,
He played with virtuosity.

But after years of harmony
She started losing her *esprit*,
And then her bridge began to crack . . .
He lost a screw, his bow went slack.
Her F-holes warped, her belly swelled,
She creaked whenever she was held.
His fiddling became erratic,
His technique merely automatic.
Appassionatas soon gave way
To rallentandos, then, no play.

One day he placed her on the shelf,
And humming softly to himself,
Put on his coat and left, hell bent,
To find a better instrument.

SAPPHO *translated by Josephine Balmer*

. . . frankly I wish that I were dead:
she was weeping as she took her leave from me

and many times she told me this:
'Oh what sadness we have suffered,
Sappho, for I'm leaving you against my will.'

So I gave this answer to her:
'Go, be happy but remember
me there, for you know how we have cherished you,

if not, then I would remind you
[of the joy we have known,] of all
the loveliness that we have shared together;

for many wreaths of violets,
of roses and of crocuses
. . . you wove around yourself by my side

. . . and many twisted garlands
which you had woven from the blooms
of flowers, you placed around your slender neck

. . . and you were anointed with
a perfume, scented with blossom,
. . . although it was fit for a queen

and on a bed, soft and tender
. . . you satisfied your desire . . .'

C. P. CAVAFY *translated by Edmund Keeley and*
Philip Sherrard

Body, Remember ...

Body, remember not only how much you were loved,
not only the beds you lay on,
but also those desires glowing openly
in eyes that looked at you,
trembling for you in voices –
only some chance obstacle frustrated them.
Now that it's all finally in the past,
it seems almost as if you gave yourself
to those desires too – how they glowed,
remember, in eyes that looked at you,
remember, body, how they trembled for you in those voices.

A Last Confession

What lively lad most pleasured me
Of all that with me lay?
I answer that I gave my soul
And loved in misery,
But had great pleasure with a lad
That I loved bodily.

Flinging from his arms I laughed
To think his passion such
He fancied that I gave a soul
Did but our bodies touch,
And laughed upon his breast to think
Beast gave beast as much.

I gave what other women gave
That stepped out of their clothes,
But when this soul, its body off,
Naked to naked goes,
He it has found shall find therein
What none other knows,

And give his own and take his own
And rule in his own right;
And though it loved in misery
Close and cling so tight,
There's not a bird of day that dare
Extinguish that delight.

GEORGE GORDON, LORD BYRON

from *Don Juan*

'They tell me 'tis decided you depart:
    'Tis wise – 'tis well, but not the less a pain;
I have no further claim on your young heart,
    Mine is the victim, and would be again:
To love too much has been the only art
    I used; – I write in haste, and if a stain
Be on this sheet, 'tis not what it appears;
My eyeballs burn and throb, but have no tears.

'I loved, I love you, for this love have lost
    State, station, heaven, mankind's, my own esteem,
And yet cannot regret what it hath cost,
    So dear is still the memory of that dream;
Yet, if I name my guilt, 'tis not to boast,
    None can deem harshlier of me than I deem:
I trace this scrawl because I cannot rest –
I've nothing to reproach or to request.

'Man's love is of man's life a thing apart,
    'Tis woman's whole existence; man may range
The court, camp, church, the vessel, and the mart;
    Sword, gown, gain, glory, offer in exchange
Pride, fame, ambition, to fill up his heart,
    And few there are whom these cannot estrange;
Men have all these resources, we but one,
To love again, and be again undone.

'You will proceed in pleasure, and in pride,
   Beloved and loving many; all is o'er
For me on earth, except some years to hide
   My shame and sorrow deep in my heart's core:
These I could bear, but cannot cast aside
   The passion which still rages as before, –
And so farewell – forgive me, love me – No,
That word is idle now – but let it go.

'My breast has been all weakness, is so yet;
   But still I think I can collect my mind;
My blood still rushes where my spirit's set,
   As roll the waves before the settled wind;
My heart is feminine, nor can forget –
   To all, except one image, madly blind;
So shakes the needle, and so stands the pole,
As vibrates my fond heart to my fix'd soul.

'I have no more to say, but linger still,
   And dare not set my seal upon this sheet,
And yet I may as well the task fulfil.
   My misery can scarce be more complete:
I had not lived till now, could sorrow kill;
   Death shuns the wretch who fain the blow would meet,
And I must even survive this last adieu,
And bear with life to love and pray for you!'

SIR THOMAS WYATT

The Forsaken Lover

They flee from me that sometime did me seek
With naked foot stalking in my chamber.
I have seen them gentle, tame and meek
That now are wild, and do not remember
That sometime they put themself in danger
To take bread at my hand; and now they range,
Busily seeking with a continual change.

Thanked be fortune, it hath been otherwise
Twenty times better, but once in special:
In thin array after a pleasant guise
When her loose gown from her shoulders did fall

And she me caught in her arms long and small
Therewithal sweetly did me kiss,
And softly said, 'Dear heart, how like you this?'

It was no dream. I lay broad waking.
But all is turned through my gentleness
Into a strange fashion of forsaking,
And I have leave to go, of her goodness,
And she also to use newfangleness.
But since that I so kindly am served,
I would fain know what she hath deserved.

THOMAS HARDY

The Ruined Maid

'O 'Melia, my dear, this does everything crown!
Who could have supposed I should meet you in Town?
And whence such fair garments, such prosperi-ty?' –
'O didn't you know I'd been ruined?' said she.

– 'You left us in tatters, without shoes or socks,
Tired of digging potatoes, and spudding up docks;
And now you've gay bracelets and bright feathers three!' –
'Yes: that's how we dress when we're ruined,' said she.

– 'At home in the barton you said "thee" and "thou",
And "thik oon", and "theäs oon", and "t'other"; but now
Your talking quite fits 'ee for high compa-ny!' –
'Some polish is gained with one's ruin,' said she.

– 'Your hands were like paws then, your face blue and
   bleak
But now I'm bewitched by your delicate cheek,
And your little gloves fit as on any la-dy!' –
'We never do work when we're ruined,' said she.

– 'You used to call home-life a hag-ridden dream,
And you'd sigh, and you'd sock; but at present you seem
To know not of megrims or melancho-ly!' –
'True. One's pretty lively when ruined,' said she.

– 'I wish I had feathers, a fine sweeping gown,
And a delicate face, and could strut about Town!' –
'My dear – a raw country girl, such as you be,
Cannot quite expect that. You ain't ruined,' said she.

JOHN DRYDEN

Prologue to *An Evening's Love*

When first our Poet set himself to write,
Like a young Bridegroom on his Wedding-night
He layd about him, and did so bestir him,
His Muse could never lye in quiet for him:
But now his Honey-moon is gone and past,
Yet the ungrateful drudgery must last:
And he is bound, as civil Husbands do,
To strain himself, in complaisance to you:
To write in pain, and counterfeit a bliss,
Like the faint smackings of an after kiss.
But you, like Wives ill pleas'd, supply his want;
Each writing Monsieur is a fresh Gallant:
And though, perhaps, 'twas done as well before,
Yet still there's something in a new amour.
Your several Poets work with several tools,
One gets you wits, another gets you fools:
This pleases you with some by-stroke of wit,
This finds some cranny, that was never hit.
But should these janty Lovers daily come
To do your work, like your good man at home,
Their fine small timber'd wits would soon decay;
These are Gallants but for a Holiday.
Others you had who oftner have appear'd,
Whom, for meer impotence you have cashier'd:
Such as at first came on with pomp and glory,
But, overstraining, soon fell flat before yee.
Their useless weight with patience long was born,
But at the last you threw 'em off with scorn.
As for the Poet of this present night,

Though now he claims in you an Husbands right,
He will not hinder you of fresh delight.
He, like a Seaman, seldom will appear;
And means to trouble home but thrice a year:
That only time from your Gallants he'll borrow;
Be kind to day, and Cuckold him to morrow.

JOHN WILMOT, EARL OF ROCHESTER

To a Lady in a Letter

Such perfect bliss, fair Cloris, we
   In our enjoyment prove,
'Tis pity restless jealousy
   Should mingle with our love.

Let us, since wit has taught us how,
   Raise pleasure to the top:
You rival bottle must allow,
   I'll suffer rival fop.

Think not in this that I design
   A treason 'gainst love's charms,
When following the god of wine
   I leave my Cloris' arms,

Since you have that, for all your haste,
   At which I'll ne'er repine,
Will take its liquor off as fast
   As I can take off mine.

There's not a brisk insipid spark
   That flutters in the town
But with your wanton eyes you mark
   Him out to be your own;

Nor do you think it worth your care
   How empty, and how dull,
The heads of your admirers are
   So that their cods be full.

All this you freely may confess,
    Yet we ne'er disagree,
For did you love your pleasure less
    You were no match for me,

Whilst I, my pleasure to pursue,
    Whole nights am taking in
The lusty juice of grapes, take you
    The juice of lusty men.

PETER READING

Midnight

                    a hotel bedroom, open window,
sibilant tyres on rain-washed asphalt streets
whispering a repetitious *finish, finish*.
You stroke your lover comprehensively,
who purrs contentment, clings to your neck and sobs.
Sibilant tyres on rain-washed asphalt streets
whispering a repetitious *finish, finish*.

Porphyria's Lover

The rain set early in to-night,
    The sullen wind was soon awake,
It tore the elm-tops down for spite,
    And did its worst to vex the lake:
    I listened with heart fit to break.
When glided in Porphyria; straight
    She shut the cold out and the storm,
And kneeled and made the cheerless grate
    Blaze up, and all the cottage warm;
    Which done, she rose, and from her form
Withdrew the dripping cloak and shawl,
    And laid her soiled gloves by, untied
Her hat and let the damp hair fall,
    And, last, she sat down by my side
    And called me. When no voice replied,
She put my arm about her waist,
    And made her smooth white shoulder bare,
And all her yellow hair displaced,
    And, stooping, made my cheek lie there,
    And spread, o'er all, her yellow hair,
Murmuring how she loved me – she
    Too weak, for all her heart's endeavour,
To set its struggling passion free
    From pride, and vainer ties dissever,
    And give herself to me for ever.
But passion sometimes would prevail,
    Nor could to-night's gay feast restrain
A sudden thought of one so pale
    For love of her, and all in vain:

So, she was come through wind and rain.
Be sure I looked up at her eyes
    Happy and proud; at last I knew
Porphyria worshipped me; surprise
    Made my heart swell, and still it grew
    While I debated what to do.
That moment she was mine, mine, fair,
    Perfectly pure and good: I found
A thing to do, and all her hair
    In one long yellow string I wound
    Three times her little throat around,
And strangled her. No pain felt she;
    I am quite sure she felt no pain.
As a shut bud that holds a bee,
    I warily oped her lids: again
    Laughed the blue eyes without a stain.
And I untightened next the tress
    About her neck; her cheek once more
Blushed bright beneath my burning kiss:
    I propped her head up as before,
    Only, this time my shoulder bore
Her head, which droops upon it still:
    The smiling rosy little head,
So glad it has its utmost will,
    That all it scorned at once is fled,
    And I, its love, am gained instead!
Porphyria's love: she guessed not how
    Her darling one wish would be heard.
And thus we sit together now,
    And all night long we have not stirred,
    And yet God has not said a word!

HUGO WILLIAMS

Message Not Left on an Answerphone

(for C.)

As night comes on, I remember we used to play
at this time of day, and you would tell me:
'Don't get excited now, or we'll miss the film.'
You would be sitting on my lap, making a fuss of me.
A shoulder strap would fall down.
A buckle would come away in my hand.
That famous buckle! Did you get it mended yet?
Sometimes the telephone would ring
while we were playing, making us cross,
even though it was still quite early.
You would pick up the phone and talk noncommittally
for a moment or two, because you had to.
How I loved you when you talked like that.
At other times we let the answerphone do the work
and listened to the names of your friends
coming through from another world.
Darling, we made ourselves late sometimes,
playing those games. We made ourselves cry.
Now it is me who hangs endlessly on the line,
who hears your voice repeating at all hours:
'I can't get to the phone at the moment,
but do leave a message.' Pick up the phone, damn you.
Can't you recognize one of my silences by now?

PAUL GROVES

Making Love to Marilyn Monroe

He pumps her up, po-faced, his right leg rising
And falling wearisomely. Breasts inflate,
Thighs fatten, force and perseverance raising
A rubber spectre. Plump, comical feet
Swell into being, but her eyes stay dead.
Her crotch arrives; exaggerated, furry.

Five minutes and she's full. Pink. Somewhat odd.
His brother brought her over on the ferry
From Hook of Holland, folded flat beneath
Shirts and trousers. Bought in Amsterdam,
She needed only an awakening breath,
Divine afflatus nurturing the dream

Till it becomes substantial. When she's tight
He plugs her with a stopper, tests for leaks
With an embrace, marvels at each huge teat,
And stands back slightly to admire her looks.
She leans against the sofa at an angle,
Legs amply parted, lips a sullen pout.

Like Mae West she might mutter, 'I'm no angel'
If able to articulate. Her pert
Expression is the only clue he'll get
To how she feels. If he but had a wand
He'd *ping* her into life, but all she's got
To offer him is quick relief and wind.

He gets it over with, lights turned down low.
Pneumatic gasps were absent. Self-esteem
Plummets, yet she was an easy lay.
He puts her in the wardrobe till next time.
The sorry fact is real women don't
Fancy him. A shrink would understand.

Who are so inflated that no dent
Disfigures them? Some men need to get stoned
Before they do it; some touch little girls . . .
At least this shady rigmarole can bring
Release without distress. Contentment gels.
Doubt punctures with a quintessential bang.

FLEUR ADCOCK

Against Coupling

I write in praise of the solitary act:
of not feeling a trespassing tongue
forced into one's mouth, one's breath
smothered, nipples crushed against the
ribcage, and that metallic tingling
in the chin set off by a certain odd nerve:

unpleasure. Just to avoid those eyes would help –
such eyes as a young girl draws life from,
listening to the vegetal
rustle within her, as his gaze
stirs polypal fronds in the obscure
sea-bed of her body, and her own eyes blur.

There is much to be said for abandoning
this no longer novel exercise –
for not 'participating in
a total experience' – when
one feels like the lady in Leeds who
had seen *The Sound of Music* eighty-six times;

or more, perhaps, like the school drama mistress
producing *A Midsummer Night's Dream*
for the seventh year running, with
yet another cast from 5B.
Pyramus and Thisbe are dead, but
the hole in the wall can still be troublesome.

I advise you, then, to embrace it without
encumbrance. No need to set the scene,
dress up (or undress), make speeches.
Five minutes of solitude are
enough – in the bath, or to fill
that gap between the Sunday papers and lunch.

LIZ LOCHHEAD

Morning After

Sad how
Sunday morning finds us
separate after All,
side by side with nothing between us
but the Sunday papers.
Held like screens before us.
    Me, the Mirror
reflecting only on your closed profile.
    You, the Observer
encompassing larger, Other issues.

Without looking up
you ask me please to pass the colour section.
I shiver
while you flick too quickly
        too casually through the pages, with
        too passing
        an interest.

A. E. HOUSMAN

Oh, When I was in Love

Oh, when I was in love with you,
   Then I was clean and brave,
And miles around the wonder grew
   How well did I behave.

And now the fancy passes by,
   And nothing will remain.
And miles around they'll say that I
   Am quite myself again.

WILLIAM SHAKESPEARE

Clown's Song

When that I was and a little tiny boy,
  With hey, ho, the wind and the rain,
A foolish thing was but a toy,
  For the rain it raineth every day.

But when I came to man's estate,
  With hey, ho, the wind and the rain,
'Gainst knaves and thieves men shut their gate,
  For the rain it raineth every day.

But when I came, alas, to wive,
  With hey, ho, the wind and the rain,
By swaggering could I never thrive,
  For the rain it raineth every day.

But when I came unto my beds,
  With hey, ho, the wind and the rain,
With tosspots still had drunken heads,
  For the rain it raineth every day.

A great while ago the world begun,
  With hey, ho, the wind and the rain;
But that's all one, our play is done,
  And we'll strive to please you every day.

ACKNOWLEDGEMENTS

The editor and publishers gratefully acknowledge permission to use copyright material in this book as follows:

Fleur Adcock: to Oxford University Press for 'Against Coupling' from *Selected Poems* (1971)

John Agard: to the author c/o Caroline Sheldon Literary Agency for 'Blessed Undressed' and 'The Lover' from *Lovelines for a Goat-born Lady* (Serpent's Tail, 1990)

Simon Armitage: to Faber & Faber Ltd for 'You May Turn Over and Begin . . .' and 'To His Lost Lover' from *Book of Matches* (1993) and *Kid* (1992)

Josephine Balmer (translator): to Bloodaxe Books Ltd for Fragments 3, 26, 27, 28, 32, 38 and 48 from *Poems & Fragments by Sappho* (Bloodaxe, 1992)

Mary Barnard (translator): to University of California Press for two poems from *Sappho: A New Translation*. Copyright © 1958 The Regents of the University of California: © renewed 1984 Mary Barnard

John Berryman: to Faber & Faber Ltd for '4th Song from 77 Dream Songs' from *Dream Songs*

Sujata Bhatt: to Carcanet Press Ltd for 'Shérdi' from *Brunizem* (1988)

C. P. Cavafy: to Random House UK Ltd for 'Come Back', 'One Night', 'Body, Remember . . .' and 'Two Young Men, 23 to 24 Years Old' from *Collected Poems*, translated by Edmund Keeley and Philip Sherrard, edited by George Savidis (Chatto and Windus, 1990)

Wendy Cope: to Faber & Faber Ltd for 'Strugnell's Sonnets' (extract) and 'Verse for a Birthday Card' from *Making Cocoa for Kingsley Amis* (Faber, 1986)

E. E. Cummings: to W. W. Norton & Company Ltd for 'she being Brand', 'may I feel said he' and 'i like my body when it is with your' from *Complete Poems* 1904–1962, edited by

Alan Jenkins: to Random House UK Ltd for 'Storm' from *Harm*
(Chatto & Windus, 1984)

Richard Jones: to the author for 'Wan Chu's Wife in Bed' from
New American Poets of the 90s (David R. Godine Publishers).
Copyright © Richard Jones, 1990

D. H. Lawrence: to Laurence Pollinger Ltd and the Estate of
Frieda Lawrence Ravagli for 'Figs', from *The Complete Poems
of D. H. Lawrence*

Liz Lochhead: to Polygon Publishers for 'After Leaving the
Castle' and 'Morning After' from *Dreaming Frankenstein*
(1984); to Penguin Books Ltd for 'Sexual Etiquette' from
Bagpipe Muzak (1991)

Federico García Lorca: to Penguin Books Ltd for 'The Faithless
Wife', translated by Stephen Spender and J. L. Gili from
Selected Poems (1960)

Edna St Vincent Millay: to A. M. Heath & Company Ltd for
'What Lips My Lips Have Kissed' from *Collected Poems*
(Harper & Row). Copyright 1923, 1951 by Edna St Vincent
Millay and Norma Millay Ellis

Kaccipēṭṭu Naṉṉākaiyār: to Peter Owen Ltd for 'My lover
capable of terrible lies' from *The Interior Landscape: Love
Poems from a Classical Tamil Anthology*, translated by A. K.
Ramanujan (Indiana University Press)

Grace Nichols: to Curtis Brown Ltd for 'Grease', 'The Decision',
'Invitation' and 'My Black Triangle' from *Lazy Thoughts of a
Lazy Woman* (Virago, 1989). Copyright © Grace Nichols
(1989)

Patrick O'Shaughnessy: to the author for 'Endpiece' from
Rapture, Rue & Ribaldry (Dolphin Lane Books, 1995)

Lynn Peters: to A. P. Watt Ltd on behalf of the author for 'I
Suspect' from *Cosmopolitan* (1986)

Fiona Pitt-Kethley: to the author for her two translations from
The Literary Companion to Sex (Sinclair-Stevenson).
Translation © Fiona Pitt-Kethley, 1992

Ezra Pound: to Faber & Faber Ltd for 'Night Song' from
Collected Shorter Poems

Rodney Pybus (translator): to the translator for 'Dearest Ipsitilla' by Catullus from the *Faber Book of Blue Verse*, edited by John Whitworth (1990)

Craig Raine: to Oxford University Press for 'Sexual Couplets' from *A Martian Sends a Postcard Home* (1979)

Peter Reading: to the author for 'Carte Postale' and 'Tryst' from *3 in 1 Diplopic* (Chatto & Windus) and 'Midnight' from *Last Poems* (Chatto & Windus)

Anne Sexton: to the Peters, Fraser & Dunlop Group Ltd for 'For My Lover, Returning to His Wife' from *Love Poems* (Cape, 1967)

Stevie Smith: to James MacGibbon for 'Infelice' from *The Collected Poems of Stevie Smith* (Penguin Twentieth Century Classics)

Arthur Symons: to William Heinemann Ltd for 'White Heliotrope' from *Victorian Verse*, edited by George MacBeth (Penguin, 1986)

Joan Van Poznak: to the author for 'Viola d'Amore' from the *Faber Book of Blue Verse* (1990)

Hugo Williams: to Oxford University Press Ltd for 'Toilet' from *Self Portrait with a Slide* (1990); to Faber & Faber Ltd for 'Prayer' and 'Message Not Left on an Answerphone' from *Dock Leaves* (1994)

Tennessee Williams: to Casarotto Ramsay Ltd for 'Life Story'

W. B. Yeats: to A. P. Watt Ltd on behalf of Michael Yeats for 'Leda and the Swan' and 'A Last Confession' from *The Collected Poems of W. B. Yeats* (Macmillan)

Every effort has been made to contact all copyright holders. The publishers would be grateful to be notified of any amendments or corrections that should be incorporated in the next edition of this volume.

INDEX OF POETS AND TRANSLATORS

INDEX OF TITLES AND FIRST LINES